TURNING POINTS

TURNING POINTS

Preeminent writers offering fresh, personal
perspectives on the defining events of our time

William Least Heat-Moon, *Columbus in the Americas*

Scott Simon, *Jackie Robinson and
the Integration of Baseball*

Alan Dershowitz, *America Declares Independence*

Thomas Fleming, *The Louisiana Purchase*

Eleanor Clift, *Founding Sisters and
the Nineteenth Amendment*

Bob Edwards, *Edward R. Murrow and
the Birth of Broadcast Journalism*

Sir Martin Gilbert, *D-Day*

Martin Goldsmith, *The Beatles Come to America*

The Fall of the Berlin Wall

Also by William F. Buckley Jr.

TURNING POINTS

The Fall of the Berlin Wall

WILLIAM F. BUCKLEY JR.

WILEY

John Wiley & Sons, Inc.

For general information about our other products and services, please contact our Customer Care Department within the United States at (800) 762-2974, outside the United
States at (317) 572-3993 or fax (317) 572-4002.

Wiley also publishes its books in a variety of electronic formats. Some content that
appears in print may not be available in electronic books. For more information about
Wiley products, visit our web site at www.wiley.com.

Library of Congress Cataloging-in-Publication Data:

Buckley, William F. (William Frank), 1925–
   The fall of the Berlin Wall / William F. Buckley.
     p. cm.
Includes bibliographical references and index.
   ISBN 0-471-26736-8 (Cloth)
   ISBN 978-0470-49668-8 (Pbk.)
   1. Berlin Wall, Berlin, Germany, 1961–1989. 2. Berlin
(Germany)—Politics and government—1945–1990. 3. Germany—
History—Unification, 1990. 4. Cold War. I. Title.
   DD881.B797 2004
   943'.1550875—dc22
                                               2003016086

Printed in the United States of America

10 9 8 7 6 5 4 3 2 1

For Linda Bridges,
friend and colleague of many years

Contents

Foreword

By Henry A. Kissinger

Bill Buckley was one of the most remarkable men of our time. Over fifty years ago, barely out of college, he rejected conventional wisdom and founded a magazine, *National Review*, dedicated to standing athwart the prevalent intellectual currents. It seemed an improbable undertaking at a time when the intellectual ramparts were close to being monopolized by the dominant liberal philosophy. Three decades later, it was his adversaries who were in retreat. Conservatives controlled Congress and elected presidents. As these lines are being written, the tide has reversed once more. But Bill Buckley's legacy endures: in the journal he created, the disciples he inspired, the values he affirmed.

Passionate in controversy, Buckley at the same time symbolized the essential unity of our society around the ideas of freedom and human dignity. No advocate in our time treated his opponents with more respect; his forensic skill was in the service of causes, not personalities. Acerbic as a debater, he was, in the end, a great unifier in our society;

the attendance at his memorial service was a testimony to the reach of his convictions and the impact of his personality.

Bill Buckley's reach reflected his versatility. Every year he produced a beautifully written book; he hosted an influential talk show for thirty years; he delivered over fifty lectures annually; he wrote important columns every week. In what passed for his spare time, he was an accomplished harpsichordist, a passionate skier, and a daring sailor. He was as close to a universal man as his generation produced.

The Fall of the Berlin Wall is an expression of Buckley's scope. Brilliantly written and extremely well researched, it sketches the creation, evolution, and demise of what became the symbol of the Cold War, of Europe's division, and of the Communist challenge to human freedom. That the Berlin Wall became so pivotal was the result of one of the anomalies of the postwar settlement. The joint occupation by the four victors—the United States, the Soviet Union, Great Britain, and France—of Germany's capital, located ninety miles inside the Soviet zone of occupation, grew out of the wartime illusion of continued allied cooperation in the governance of a defeated Germany.

The premise was bound to be unfulfilled. Stalin saw in victory an opportunity to combine historic Russian imperialism with Communist ideology and insisted on installing Soviet-style governments in what he treated as Russia's sphere in Central and Eastern Europe up to the Elbe River. The principal states in that region—Poland, Hungary,

Czechoslovakia, and, in its way, Germany—had been key participants in Western history for centuries and shared many of the West's fundamental values. To maintain dominance, the Soviet Union felt obliged to suppress all vestiges of independence and any political movement that deviated from Moscow's line. But it never succeeded in establishing governments that were accepted by their populations. Moscow lacked the values to turn the Central Europeans into willing adherents to the Soviet model. Despite the apparatus of the police state, a series of uprisings broke out—in East Germany in 1953, in Hungary in 1956, in Czechoslovakia in 1968—that could be put down only by the Soviet army. Poland, the largest of the so-called satellite states, was in a condition of incipient revolt in 1956 and then again with the emergence of the Solidarity movement in the 1970s, requiring Soviet forces to stand by in readiness to intervene.

After the occupation of Czechoslovakia in 1968, Leonid Brezhnev, then Party Secretary, proclaimed a doctrine named after himself, according to which the Soviet Union would not permit the overthrow of any Communist regime once established. (The possible application of the Brezhnev Doctrine to China proved to be one of the reasons for Mao's willingness to begin negotiations with the United States.)

As it turned out, the imposition of ideologically acceptable leaders in Eastern Europe did not end Soviet dilemmas. For these leaders found that unless they wanted to govern with Soviet bayonets, they needed to appeal to the historic legitimizing principle of nationalism, linked now to some degree of democratization. This gradual, almost imperceptible, process was to undermine Soviet rule over the next twenty years.

Of all the satellites, the so-called German Democratic Republic (GDR) in the eastern part of Germany was in the most complicated position. It represented no historic entity; the division of Germany ran counter to established national feelings. Unlike the satellites farther east, it could be reached by Western—especially German—television, so that the people could see the difference in living conditions for themselves. The existence of the western part of Berlin as a de facto part of West Germany provided a symbol and, above all, an escape route for the disaffected. The growing number of refugees threatened to drain the country of its talents.

The Soviet Union sought to counteract these trends with periodic attempts at intimidation in the form of ultimatums threatening to cut access routes to Berlin, turning it into a free city and severing its political links to the Federal Republic. But in the end, Moscow always recoiled from the confrontation that such actions would have entailed. It opted for building the wall, a human atrocity but a retreat from the Soviets' basic demands.

From that point, the wall became a symbol of Communist inhumanity and historic irrelevancy. A state claiming international recognition could maintain itself only by turning its citizens into prisoners.

At first, the wall also brought new perplexities to the Western alliance. It destroyed the myth that strengthening Western defenses and unity would lead automatically to a collapse of Europe's dividing line. It brought into sharp relief that there was a gap between West Germany and its allies on the issue of German unification. Chancellor Konrad Adenauer had made the heroic decision to give the Western alliance precedence over unification. But as each crisis evolved, allied priorities emerged as not identical. For West Germany's allies, unification was an objective affirmed to maintain the support of a valued partner; it was not an inner necessity. For West Germany, over a historic period, it would be the test of the validity of its overall strategy. The Western allies saw in the wall a challenge to the freedom of West Berlin; however, they were prepared to run few risks to restore the unity of Berlin, on which they had agreed at the end of the war.

But German leaders could not sustain so passive an approach. They sought other options, culminating in the so-called Ostpolitik, seeking to achieve national goals by direct dealings with the Soviet Union. Though some in the West—including this writer—were at first disquieted by the prospect of a German national option toward the East, the inherent dilemmas of the Soviet position led to a gradual weakening of long-term Soviet prospects. The Kremlin could achieve ratification of Ostpolitik in the West German parliament only by making a new agreement with the Western allies on Berlin, which removed previous possibilities of harassment. The evolution of Central Europe turned gradually into a Soviet rearguard action secured by progressive concessions to Central and East European national sentiments and increased self-government.

The ultimate irony was that by the time the wall came

down, it had been made irrelevant by the actions of other satellite states, specifically Hungary and Czechoslovakia. These two allies of the German Democratic Republic refused to accept the premise of the wall and permitted East German refugees in their countries to move on to West Germany. Henceforth, the GDR could have hung onto its citizens only by building a wall around the entire country.

Bill Buckley traces these events in his customary readable manner, enhancing the inherent drama with sketches of the personalities involved and the internal deliberations of the various parties, reflecting an extraordinary research effort.

In June 1990, I had the privilege of filming a *Firing Line* program with Bill in Berlin. It was his first visit since the wall had come down—an experience that went into the writing of this book. We had a drink together and engaged in some melancholy reflections on what America might have done at various earlier points—in 1948 or 1953, or in 1956, 1961, or 1968—to accelerate the ending of Soviet domination, and how many lives might have been saved. But it was also possible that the totality of the Soviet collapse required a certain evolution and the ultimate uprising of the captive peoples.

Bill returns to these questions in concluding his narrative. He leaves it to the reader to draw his or her own conclusions. He leaves no doubt what role he would have preferred his country to play.

Acknowledgments

I am indebted to Hana Lane, my editor at John Wiley & Sons, for coming up with the idea for this book on the fall (preceded by the rise) of the Berlin Wall. She was certain such a book was needed, and I hope she is proved correct. My agent, Lois Wallace, was an enthusiast for the enterprise, and of course she is correct about everything. The book would have been impossible without the research and patience and diligence and spirit of Linda Bridges, to whom I happily dedicate *The Fall of the Berlin Wall*.

—WFB
Stamford, Connecticut, July 2003

Introduction

I came to Berlin as a city that figured in any direct way in my life late, in 1983, when I undertook to write a novel about the rise of the wall. In the book, I took a few liberties with history but none that got in the way of the basic drama of the day in August 1961 when the wall started growing up as if it had for one thousand years been fed by geological and vegetable growths now bursting forth. That, looking back, is what the wall seemed: an outcropping of parthenogenic substance, just—rising, a fortress to keep East Germany's legions in the fold.

Of course, the wall was very much man-made, and the details are all in this book. The critical detail for my novel *(The Story of Henri Tod)* was the warning given by First Secretary Nikita Khrushchev to Walter Ulbricht, the ruler of the German Democratic Republic. What Khrushchev said was: *We Soviets are willing to risk giving the impression that we are prepared to use force against the West; what we are* not *willing to risk is a major engagement with the West.* This meant, in the view of some who studied the rise of the wall, that if a show of U.S. tanks had challenged the wall-builders—had run down the barbed-wire stakeouts—

Soviet tanks would not have moved forward to counter this assertion of joint occupation rights in Berlin. Henri Tod, the heroic resistance leader in my novel, was all set to do exactly that: move forward a couple of U.S. tanks, diverted from the armory by young German patriot engineers. But reality moved in, aborting the enterprise while my CIA agent, Blackford Oakes, was tied up in a cellar. What a fancy!

But the best fancies work—would have worked, if you had just closed your eyes for a minute and let truth and justice and liberty move the chess pieces.

Well, the wall went up, and, as history shows, the reaction of the West was pretty dead, acquiescent. We came to know that John Kennedy and Harold Macmillan and Charles de Gaulle were actually relieved. They had feared that Khrushchev's bluster, which had been raging all that year, threatened something worse than merely closing down traffic from East Berlin to West Berlin. They feared the Soviets would threaten West Berlin itself.

The suspense one might then have anticipated—How long will the wall last?—was itself deadened. There was little life in the movement to free East Berlin. I attended occasional gatherings of the Captive Nations Committee in New York City, which would now and then bring in a man or woman from Europe to remind as many Americans as could be got to hear the story about life in Berlin, like life elsewhere in Eastern Europe. The talk was vivid of the privations of Berliners, but not of any forthcoming relief.

In 1970 I found myself with credentials sufficient to effect a visit and presented myself at Checkpoint Charlie. I had been appointed to the U.S. Advisory Commission on

Information with warrants to go anywhere I wished to go, in fulfillment of obligations to advise the U.S. Information Agency. I submitted to the formalities of passage. My diplomatic passport was useful, but the Vopos (the East German police) stalled me for a full twenty minutes in the little compound, a way of saying that although formal diplomatic concessions were being made, there was no reason for the visitor not to feel the heavy heel of the commanding entity, the German Democratic Republic. I don't conceal that I thought the Germans who were enforcing the laws appeared especially well qualified to do so, in the square-set resolution of their heads, the grimness of their expressions, and their disembodied attention to bureaucratic duty. I never met a live Nazi, but I was experiencing treatment by sons of Nazis who had been very much alive twenty-five years earlier.

I wrote about my visit to Berlin and from time to time about Berlin as what always seemed a very conspicuous linchpin to that enslaved region of the postwar world. What I never did was reason fruitfully to what exactly would be required to bring the wall down. I am glad I did not attempt to do this, because I would not have been able to write with anything like the authority now made possible, thanks to the work of so many historians and journalists and diplomats who have told their stories.

I write that the Berlin Wall came down owing to the finally undeniable spirit of East German dissenters. That's true. But they were helped along by the final, liberating equivocation of the Communist overlords. No doubt there are still last-ditch East Berlin Communists, in their fifties and sixties and seventies, who nourish their own forlorn fancies, notably that if Moscow had not lost its will . . . Yes, and if the dissenters had been more forcefully contained, not only in Berlin, but also in Warsaw, Prague, Budapest, Sofia. The fall of the wall was a vindication also of the West, especially of such Westerners as Ronald Reagan and Margaret Thatcher, because the West maintained an iron echelon, way back then, that the Kremlin could not ignore in devising workable strategic movements.

In my novel, the young protagonist actually works for Walter Ulbricht, because he is a twenty-one-year-old nephew for whose orphanage Ulbricht had direct responsibility. Young Caspar and his girlfriend, Claudia, happen on a deserted railroad car in the forest of abandoned cars in a mammoth Berlin train station. This one, unrecognized by the guards on routine duty in the great yard, was special. It was Adolf Hitler's private railroad car, and in it Caspar and Claudia nurse the wounded Henri Tod. And there they plot the diversion of three U.S. tanks for the Sunday the wall will go up, the date and hour known to the nephew of Walter Ulbricht, who clocks in every day to do his clerical work.

Less than one hour after midnight on August 13, 1961, cross-border traffic is halted, the East German army rolls down Unter den Linden, and the young plotters are bloodily executed. They would sleep twenty-eight years before the wall came down, rising then with so many others in the community of the dead, to take heart that history had turned, finally, in their favor. Ilya Ehrenburg wrote that when all the world is surfaced over in concrete, one day a blade of grass will sprout up. This happened in Berlin on November 9, 1989.

1

Ulbricht's Berlin Problem

Early in the year in which John F. Kennedy became president of the United States, apprehension about Soviet foreign policy was high. Nikita Khrushchev was in power, and his rhetoric was threatening. Historians looking back on the crisis centering on Berlin, 1961, now mostly agree that it was not on the scale of what would come one year later over Soviet missiles in Cuba, but at the time, Khrushchev's claims, and the bellicose language he used in pressing them, made it sound as if World War III were imminent.

The threat by the noisy first secretary, boss of the Soviet Union and of the Eastern European Communist world, was that he was prepared to write a separate peace treaty with East Germany. The situation Khrushchev was exploiting was the result of what Stalin, Churchill, and Roosevelt had agreed upon at Yalta in February 1945. What they had done there was confirmed and embellished at the Potsdam conference in July and August 1945 and expanded in sub-agreements over the ensuing months. The design was to invest formal authority over Germany in the victorious powers: Soviet, British, and American. To their number France was added, with the war's end, something of a collegial gesture by Britain and the United States. These powers would jointly govern Germany and, within it, Berlin. For administrative purposes, Germany was divided into four zones, Berlin into four sectors, each assigned to one of the occupying powers. But it was assumed that the four powers would make policy jointly, and that the personnel of each of them, military and civilian, would have unimpeded access to all four sectors and zones.

The Soviets had unilaterally violated these understandings from the outset. They began to make their own policies in the part of Germany, and of Berlin, that they controlled, without a nod of the head to their co-responsible allies. Early in 1948, the Soviets stopped even dispatching a representative to joint occupation meetings. At that point the Western occupying powers, which believed it was time to start gradually devolving upon all of Germany the authority to rule itself, decided to go ahead with the part under *their* control. This had approximately 51 million inhabitants, as against 16 million for the part under Soviet control.

The West Germans were now allowed to set up their own parliament, but it would still be a long apprenticeship back to sovereignty. They had no authority to mobilize an army or to make policies that had military implications. The American representative in Bonn was still called the U.S. high commissioner, retaining plenary contingent authority. Not until 1954 did the Western powers grant substantial sovereignty to the Federal Republic of Germany, the high commissioner becoming, simply, ambassador.

In 1949 the Soviet Union granted ostensible authority to the German Democratic Republic—ostensible, because the GDR was of course a satellite nation. Walter Ulbricht, who had been the third-ranking member of the original government of occupied East Germany, rose quickly to de facto chief of government. His formal portfolio was secretary-general of the Central Committee, the counterpart of Stalin's and then Khrushchev's ranking in the Soviet Union. He was also deputy premier, but, as Moscow's man, he wielded far more power than the actual premier, Otto Grotewohl, or President Wilhelm Pieck.

A divided Germany and a divided Berlin, formally under occupation authority, was still the status quo as of 1958, when Khrushchev first threatened to sign a separate peace treaty with East Germany. Whenever he or his spokesmen elucidated on the point, they reasoned that World War II was long since over, and therefore there was no need to hold Germany in subjugated status. Why should we not, Khrushchev asked, proceed to make a final settlement?

This was more or less what the Allies had argued in 1954. What was different, and alarming, was the Kremlin's attitude on Berlin. When, in November 1958, Khrushchev announced his plan for East German sovereignty, he made it clear that he was not only talking about the Soviet Zone. He was also talking about all of Berlin. Under his plan, West Berlin would become a "free city," and authority over it would reside solely in the GDR. Khrushchev conveyed through Foreign Minister Andrei Gromyko, the grim successor to the grim Vyacheslav Molotov, that he would give the West six months to respond to his request for negotiations. If nothing was accomplished by what counted down to May 1959, Moscow would proceed with the entirely reasonable next step, which would be unilateral recognition of the German Democratic Republic as a free and sovereign state.

Khrushchev added his characteristic rhetorical flourishes at a celebration in Moscow honoring First Secretary Wladyslaw Gomulka of Poland. On that occasion, Khrushchev asserted that West Berlin was not really what it appeared to be, one half of a great city administered under the aegis of France, Great Britain, and the United States. What it had become was a Cold War fortress. Not exactly a military staging area, though there were of course military forces in the Western sectors, as permitted by the four-power agreements. No, his complaint was not of a military buildup, but that West Berlin had become a launching pad for subversives bent on weakening East Germany. Khrushchev hedged his declaration by reassuring the world that the Soviet Union had no intention of using military force over the Berlin issue. However, he immediately added, if the West should elect to engage in hostile activity, the aggressors would be "crushingly repulsed."

Berlin was well shaped by history and topography for its role in the Cold War. It is a great, sprawling city, 344 square miles, eight times the size of Paris, three times the size of London. Its perimeter would encircle the five boroughs of New York City.

Berlin turned out this way only in part because of organic growth. The decisive event in the city's aggrandizement was the annexation in 1920, under the Weimar government, of dozens of surrounding towns, villages, and estates into one administrative unit. Greater Berlin now had not just one but two rivers, the Spree and the Havel, and canals linking them. Within the city limits were the Berlin Forest, the Green Woods (Grünewald), and many acres of land suitable for orchards and truck farming. In all, a third of Berlin was, and still is, covered with parkland, forest, farmland, rivers, or lakes.

As European capitals go, Berlin is comparatively new. The first permanent settlements, along what is now Museum Island, in the eastern part of the city, date only from 1237—a dozen or more centuries after the beginnings of many other European cities. Berlin grew slowly, set back by outbreaks of the Black Death, as also by devastating wars. Only a handful of buildings from the medieval and Renaissance periods survived the Thirty Years' War (1618–1648).

The flowering of the city began at the end of that war, under the Great Elector, Friedrich Wilhelm von Hohenzollern. It was he who envisioned a wide avenue leading westward from his castle. For aesthetic reasons, as well as for comfort in the summer, he planted trees along it. The avenue thus formed became the heralded Unter den Linden—Under the Linden Trees. Walking down that avenue in 1970, I thought, however wistfully, of a walk down the Champs-Elysées, both of them central, well laid out, leafy, but, in Berlin, neglected.

Friedrich Wilhelm's successors were great builders, turning Berlin into a baroque city. Among the most notable of the new structures was Schloss Charlottenburg, which Friedrich I of Prussia ordered built some three miles to the west of the city center as a country retreat for his queen, Sophie Charlotte. In their day, at the end of the

Key

1. Havel River
2. Tegel Airport
3. East Germans' Pankow compound
4. Spree River
5. Bornholmerstrasse border crossing
6. Bernauerstrasse
7. Reichstag
8. Schloss Charlottenburg
9. Tiergarten
10. Gatow Airport
11. Kurfürstendamm
12. Potsdamerplatz
13. Brandenburg Gate
14. Under den Linden
15. Checkpont Charlie (Friedrichstrasse)
16. Museum Island
17. City Hall
18. Tempelhof Airport
19. Landwehr Canal
20. Stasi headquarters
21. Karlshorst (Soviet headquarters)
22. Glienecke Bridge
23. Steinstücken
24. U.S. Mission
25. Allied Kommandantur
26. Marienfelde refugee center
27. Teltow Canal
28. Schönefeld Airfield

seventeenth century, the royal party would have traveled from their main castle down Unter den Linden and through a large hunting preserve to reach Schloss Charlottenburg. In the eighteenth century, that hunting preserve became a park, the Tiergarten, and the Brandenburg Gate was erected at the point where Unter den Linden comes up against the eastern edge of the Tiergarten. This immense gate, six columns topped with a chariot drawn by four horses, was modeled on the entrance to the Acropolis and became the universally recognized symbol of Berlin.

In the late nineteenth century, Chancellor Bismarck was busy conquering Prussia's neighbors in order to turn the Kingdom of Prussia into an empire and his king into Kaiser Wilhelm. Shops, restaurants, and offices were built near the Tiergarten, the first large-scale expansion of Berlin west of the Brandenburg Gate. The Kurfürstendamm (near the western end of the Tiergarten) and Potsdamerplatz (to the south of the Tiergarten's eastern end) became new centers of Berlin life. This shifting of the city's center of gravity was ratified by the construction of the Reichstag at the northeastern corner of the Tiergarten.

Berliners suffered greatly from the defeat of Germany in World War I, though their city's buildings were not much damaged. And then came Adolf Hitler, and World War II.

The British air raids began in 1940; the American, in 1942. Potsdamerplatz was taken out early, reduced to rubble by a bombing raid in 1941. The Reich buildings and older official buildings nearby, along Unter den Linden, were particular targets. But it was not the Allies who destroyed the original linden trees: that had been done before the war, on Hitler's orders, to facilitate the digging of a new U-bahn (subway) tunnel. The area around the Kurfürstendamm also was hit hard. Block after block of apartment houses had their habitable areas reduced to basement and sometimes ground floor, which survivors of the air raids shared with the rats. In April 1945, one and a half million Soviet soldiers marched in from the east, determined to take revenge for the Battle of Stalingrad and the siege of Leningrad. By the time Hitler killed himself in his bunker, some fifty thousand Berliners had died and many times that number had fled; 39 percent of all buildings in the city had been destroyed, including more than a quarter of the housing stock.

When Berlin was divided among the four occupying powers, the new inter-sector borders followed the lines of the old administrative districts, so that the East–West border zigzagged wildly, sometimes going almost due north–south (as at the Brandenburg Gate), sometimes almost due east–west (as at what would become Checkpoint Charlie), sometimes curving to follow a river or canal. The Soviet Sector wound up with the historic part of Berlin—Museum Island, Unter den Linden, the Brandenburg Gate. Most of the Third Reich buildings, including the bunker, lay just southeast of the Brandenburg Gate. The Western sectors got the Tiergarten and the Reichstag, Charlottenburg and most of the forests, the Kurfürstendamm and both the existing airports, plus the land where a third airport was planned.

There was, in law, no such thing as "West Berlin" and "East Berlin," but, as with Germany as a whole, the Soviets very soon made the portion under their control separate from the other occupation sectors. West Berlin from the start was an island in the sea of the Soviet empire. In 1948 Stalin decided to sink that island by imposing a blockade on all goods coming into the western part of the city. He succeeded in stopping all road, rail, and barge traffic from West Germany. What saved West Berlin was the U.S. airlift, and what made the airlift possible was that 1920 decision to fold surrounding land into Greater Berlin. Tempelhof and Gatow airports were both small, but their existence permitted the airlift to begin immediately. Under the urging of the American military governor, General Lucius D. Clay, who organized the airlift, a third airport, Tegel, was finished in half the time projected. West Berliners had a rough few months, but the city survived, and in May 1949 Stalin gave up. Twelve years later, West Berlin was still, to Nikita Khrushchev, a "bone in my throat."

Secretary-General Walter Ulbricht was not just a Communist apparatchik, he was also a true believer. As a young man in Leipzig before World War I, he had joined Karl Liebknecht and Rosa Luxemburg's Spartacus Society. At age twenty-six, in 1919, he was a founder of the German Communist Party. He was spotted for his zeal and called to Moscow, in the mid-1920s, for training in cell organization, which he put into practice back home for the next several years, until Hitler took power in 1933. At that point, wanting to preserve their asset, the Soviet high command spirited him out of Germany. He spent most of the next twelve years in Moscow, except for a stint in Spain during that country's civil war. When he returned to Germany in 1945, he held the rank of colonel in the Red Army and served under Marshal Georgi Zhukov, chief of the Soviet General Staff.

Ulbricht greatly admired Lenin, including his goatee, causing him to grow his own in historical deference. Ulbricht bore some physical resemblance to his hero, but it wasn't enough. Where Lenin looked ruthless, Ulbricht looked disapproving. To see him standing at a lectern—shoulders squared, eyes narrowed behind steel-rimmed glasses, lips pursed above the goatee—you might take him for a solemn symphony orchestra conductor, prepared to bring down his baton on the music stand to reprimand an erring violinist. You would not immediately guess that his favored means of registering displeasure were indeterminate jail sentences and, for star transgressors, the firing squad. A nonsmoker and nondrinker (except to toast the occasional victory of the Workers' and Peasants' State, as the GDR was nicknamed), he was undeviating in doing his daily calisthenics and taking his daily run.

The admiration he had for Lenin, and then for Stalin, did not carry over to their successors. He found them lamentably unreliable, sometimes outright deviationist. Even Stalin had delayed in authorizing Ulbricht to implement a Five-Year Plan for East Germany. You cannot have a planned economy without a plan, Ulbricht complained.

Finally, in 1950, he was given the go-ahead. In July 1952 he proudly launched his first collectivization drive. It was followed, as such efforts tend to be, by serious food shortages. Ulbricht bristled at the restiveness of his people. He asked himself, What would Comrade Stalin have done in such straits? Stalin, too, had faced opposition to collectivization, in 1933, but had never been deflected from true

Communist principles. And so, instead of easing up, Ulbricht tightened the screws. The westward march began. Tens of thousands of East Germans made their way to the West.

On June 10, 1953, Ulbricht raised production quotas for factory and construction workers by a whopping 10 percent. East German workers did not have the machinery or the raw materials to make possible such an increase, even if they had had the energy. Ulbricht had that figured out. If the quota was a hundred units and an individual worker produced ninety units, his wages were correspondingly reduced.

The first reaction came on June 11, when the trade union at a construction site in East Berlin called a twenty-four-hour strike. Ulbricht did not blink. On the 15th, construction workers at another site demanded a meeting with Prime Minister Grotewohl. Instead, the Party sent representatives to factories and construction sites to explain the new quotas to the workers. The representatives were shouted and whistled into silence.

On the morning of Tuesday, June 16, workers in East Berlin started marching toward government and Party offices. When they reached Central Committee headquarters, just south of Unter den Linden, they found trucks with loudspeakers sending out Party propaganda. They demolished two of the trucks and commandeered a third, from which they broadcast their own slogans. These included, "WE DEMAND FREE ELECTIONS AND A UNITED BERLIN." When government officials refused to meet with them, the leaders of the demonstration called for a general strike the following day.

Neither the Ulbricht regime nor the East Berlin contingent of the Soviet MVD (predecessor of the KGB) was at all prepared for the workers' refusal to be cowed, or for the widespread popular support they received. The Red Army was more alert. Although Stalin had died only three months earlier and there was confusion in the Kremlin, the machinery of repression was not laggard. Moscow ordered troops to Berlin from all over East Germany.

On the morning of Wednesday, the 17th, the general strike began. It quickly turned into a riot as workers burned Soviet flags and attempted to storm government and Party buildings. Then the Soviet troops went into action. By nightfall, the first serious uprising in Eastern Europe since the Iron Curtain descended had been put down. The official casualty count was sixteen dead and another hundred-plus injured; the count eventually derived by the CIA was three hundred dead—shot, or run over by T-34 tanks—and more than a thousand injured. Riots broke out in other East German cities over the next two days, but they were smothered as quickly.

In his report to Moscow on Wednesday morning, Colonel Ivan Fadeikin, the acting MVD chief in Berlin, stated that "among the strikers there is the impression that the authorities will not resort to force because Berlin is under four-power control. If military force is used, Western tanks will come to their aid." In fact, the CIA was as surprised as the MVD, and by the time CIA Berlin got through to Washington to report on the uprising, it was over. Western public opinion scarcely noticed. The news from Berlin was overshadowed by the impending truce in the Korean War and the execution of the Rosenbergs.

Walter Ulbricht would remain in power for another two decades. By the spring of 1961 his single, obsessive aim was to keep his people from fleeing.

For all that the diplomatic and journalistic worlds knew that the West was dealing, in Eastern Europe, with a Soviet monolith, formal distinctions were carefully observed. No one questioned the decisive authority of Moscow, yet the Eastern European states—East Germany, Poland, Hungary, Czechoslovakia, Romania, and Bulgaria—had their own governments.

The men in power in those states convened from time to time at meetings of the Warsaw Pact, which, starting in 1955, bound their countries formally together. At such meetings, historians would later learn—and continue to learn as research on the secret diplomacy of the Communist world comes to light—satellite leaders with varying concerns and priorities ventilated these. Decisions were always tacitly subject to the rule of Moscow, but the satellite leaders had to listen to, and give their opinion on, proposals by sister states. In 1959, and again in 1960 and 1961, the voice of Walter Ulbricht was the most clamorous, owing to his escalating refugee problem. In 1959 an average of 7,500 East Germans a month applied for asylum at the Marienfelde refugee center in West Berlin. In 1960 that number rose to 12,600 a month. Ulbricht told his colleagues that the GDR could not live with the continuing human drainage.

Back in November 1958, when Khrushchev issued his ultimatum concerning East Germany, Ulbricht announced it to his people with great fanfare. But West Germany's chancellor Konrad Adenauer simply ignored the ultimatum. May 1959 came and went, and Khrushchev still took no active steps toward fulfilling his diplomatic initiative. Had Western resistance prevailed? In May 1960 Khrushchev formally called off the ultimatum, now eighteen months old. Addressing a political rally in East Berlin, he said, "We are realists and will not pursue an adventurous policy."

Then nine months later, on February 17, 1961, Khrushchev addressed a memorandum to Adenauer. It was past time, Khrushchev wrote, to end the postwar occupation regime. Moscow offered Bonn a choice: Take a seat at the negotiating table. By doing so, Bonn would exercise "broad opportunities for safeguarding its interests in West Berlin." That, or wait and negotiate directly with a newly sovereign East German government, without any mediating Soviet presence.

An agreeable aspect of the Khrushchev memorandum was its tone, which was uncommonly civil. For that reason, Adenauer this time didn't simply ignore the Soviet pronouncement. He acknowledged the memorandum but advised that he would need to consult his allies before replying to it in any detail. That gesture by Adenauer prompted a flurry of high-level visits.

Harold Macmillan, prime minister of Great Britain—tall, old Etonian, learned; former head of the Macmillan publishing company; an intimate of Winston Churchill, for whom he discharged important missions during the war— was the last Edwardian. He had succeeded Anthony Eden after the fiasco of Suez, when, in the fall of 1956, Great Britain, France, and Israel colluded unsuccessfully to unseat Nasser of Egypt, running into the resistance of President Eisenhower, who was campaigning for reelection. It was a crowded two weeks that included the Israeli invasion of Egypt, the Hungarian uprising, and the U.S. election. Now, in April 1961, Macmillan flew to Washington for his first formal meeting with the young, alluring John Fitzgerald Kennedy, freshly inaugurated as Eisenhower's successor.

Macmillan was apprehensive about the new, unknown American president, son of Joseph Kennedy, who as ambassador to Great Britain had counseled President Roosevelt to follow an isolationist foreign policy. Macmillan had been a friend and admirer of General Eisenhower, subsequently President Eisenhower. Deeply read in history, Macmillan felt the responsibility to continue to cultivate the Special Relationship, that deep mooring of Anglo-American friendship that permitted so much to be taken for granted, as a common language flowered into common purposes. The disruption of Suez, when President Eisenhower denied critical help to what was judged an act of arrant colonialism, had cooled the Special Relationship but hardly ended it, Winston Churchill still alive and, in his coony way, casting his eyes on the coveted alliance.

What Macmillan wanted, in the present situation, was to temporize—to stretch the Berlin crisis out, hoping that the attenuation would dissipate the threat of diplomatic convulsion. He was relieved to learn that JFK had come to roughly the same conclusion, relieved also to find the young president personally congenial. "It is curious," Macmillan later wrote in his memoirs, "how all American statesmen begin by trying to treat Britain as just one of many foreign or NATO countries. They soon find themselves relying on our advice and experience. President Kennedy and Secretary Rusk have found this out very quickly." (Dean Rusk, Georgia-born and Oxford-educated, with clerical features and manners, had been president of the Rockefeller Foundation when JFK named him secretary of state.)

Macmillan was not the only traveler. Dean Acheson, urbane, experienced, secretary of state for President Truman, now served as a special envoy of the new president. On April 9 he flew to Bonn to meet with Adenauer.

The stolid eighty-five-year-old German had survived Hitler to find himself, as the state evolved, chief of government of the western portion of postwar Germany. He was a Rhinelander, stiffly remote from the Prussians and Brandenburgers associated with Berlin, the traditional capital, Hitler's capital. A few days after Acheson's visit, Adenauer went to Washington to meet with Kennedy and subsequently to Paris to meet with President Charles de Gaulle.

Le Grand Charles was the most naturally imperious man of the age. Six feet, four inches tall, he towered over most visitors, giving an impression of hauteur and authority that he did not strive to soften. He was more old-school even than Macmillan, imperturbability being his most conspicuous characteristic. He was more than once the target of an assassination attempt by members of the Organisation de l'Armée Secrète, seeking to avenge his tergiversation on Algeria: he had begun by pronouncing it a department of France, and ended by granting it independence. After one of these attempts, the bullet having gone by, he left his car to confer with his security guards. He then walked back to his car, where his wife sat, and asked, "Vous êtes bien, madame?"

De Gaulle was acutely conscious that the liberation of France had been effected, in 1944–45, by the British and the Americans, not by the French themselves, and he fretted under the dominant American role in NATO. He would take to referring to the Soviet Union and the United States as two "hegemonies," both vying for control of Europe. He had known Macmillan since wartime days in London. On achieving power again in 1958, he tried to enlist his old friend in moves to rupture the American "hegemony." Macmillan turned de Gaulle down. The two senior statesmen remained on cordial terms, although, we would learn from de Gaulle's memoirs, he concluded regretfully that the Englishman was, intellectually, nothing much more, really, than another "Anglo-Saxon."

It was different between de Gaulle and Adenauer. De Gaulle wasn't in power when, in 1954, Adenauer was invited to visit Paris, the great, dramatic affirmation of the end of the war, with the memories of occupied France. Adenauer's host was Prime Minister Pierre Mendès-France, and during that visit de Gaulle stayed away, reclusive in his country nest at Colombey-les-Deux-Eglises, 140 miles from Paris. He waited there, but the emanations from Colombey and from de Gaulle loyalists were unmistakable. He would wait there until his countrymen showed the good sense to summon him back to the throne.

This they did in 1958, and he took immediate and comprehensive command, overseeing, even, a change in the French Constitution, so that now it was the Fifth Republic, the Third Republic having gone up in the flames of the world war, the Fourth Republic, in the bureaucratic and factionalist turmoil from which de Gaulle was called back to rescue a country in distress.

Soon afterward he invited Adenauer to Colombey for their first meeting. De Gaulle bore no suspicion of Adenauer, who had consistently registered his opposition to the bitterest enemy of France, Adolf Hitler. De Gaulle did envy the robust longevity of his West German counterpart. When de Gaulle came back to power, he was sixty-seven; Adenauer had just won reelection at eighty-one. Before Adenauer's visit, de Gaulle had remarked to an aide, "I've come back ten years too late." Now he asked Adenauer: How had he managed to cope with aging? Der Alte (the Old Man, as he was universally known) replied that the explanation for his continued health, personal and political, was as simple as that he had "broken the age barrier"; he could now go on indefinitely. De Gaulle was drawn to the formulation, and happily told everyone he met, "J'ai franchi la barrière d'âge."

The unification of Germany had been effected in 1871, under Kaiser Wilhelm I and the iron-willed Bismarck. Five years later, Konrad Adenauer was born in Cologne, where he lived under the rule of the kaisers and practiced law. When World War I broke out, he was serving as mayor of Cologne. In 1933, life under Hitler began.

Adenauer was in and out of Hitler's jails during the dozen years of Nazi rule. Most of the time he was under house arrest, living in his beloved Rhöndorf, a village with a dramatic view of the Rhine, midway between Cologne and Bonn. The single activity in which he was not molested by the superintending Nazi guards was gardening, to which he devoted himself assiduously, while piecing together news of the vicissitudes of war from radio broadcasts. With Hitler's defeat, he reentered politics and rose quickly to become president of the Parliamentary Council deputized to draft a Basic Law (essentially a constitution) for the Western zones—British, French, and American. The Basic Law was promulgated in May 1949, and in September Adenauer became chancellor.

West Germany's cities were crushed from the years of intense bombing; the poverty was drastic, the torrent of refugees from East Germany, enormous, totaling nearly 4 million in the decade after the war. The Nazi leaders had been tried at Nuremberg, which yielded some satisfaction, but their hanging did nothing to alleviate the economic misery. Inflation had appeared uncheckable until the currency reform of 1948, initiated by Adenauer's economic director, Ludwig Erhard.

At home, the disheveled cities. To the east, the enslaved sister state. The ancient capital of Berlin lay seventy-five miles deep in East Germany. The West Germans rigorously upheld the notion that Berlin was their true capital and Bonn was merely an expedient, pending free elections in the East and the country's reunification.

So, Adenauer's government looked forward to a renascent Berlin but devoted its energies to a renascent West Germany. And inch by inch, going to leaps and bounds, Adenauer made his way, simultaneously rebuilding the reputation of his country by his massive, incorruptible solidity. When Mendès-France invited him to Paris, postwar

Germany was psychologically recognized, the rule of Hitler consigned to a gruesome historical misadventure.

Georges Clemenceau had cracked wryly at the Versailles Conference of 1919, which plundered the vanquished enemy and sprouted Hitler, that he thought so highly of Germany he believed there should be at least two of them. That was an early vision of a permanently disabled Germany, which was renewed in discussions toward the end of World War II on what to do *this* time to tame Germany. Henry Morgenthau Jr., FDR's treasury secretary, believed that Germany could never be trusted unless it was reduced to an agricultural state, shorn of industrial power. But the Morgenthau plan was not adopted by FDR, and by 1954 there was no sense, except in Soviet rhetoric, that the bloodlines that had created Hitler were still alive in the country governed by Der Alte.

The Western leaders reacted predictably to Khrushchev's ultimatum on Berlin. Adenauer pointed out that to negotiate with the Soviet Union meant to acknowledge a hypothesis: namely, that there was something the Allies were prepared to give up. Since that was not the case, there was, Q.E.D., no point in negotiating. De Gaulle weighed the question and himself concluded that the two sides' positions were mutually exclusive. He joined with Adenauer: no negotiations.

Harold Macmillan, on the other hand, an empiricist by disposition, was inclined to negotiation rather than confrontation, and JFK had come to the same conclusion, at least at one level. Macmillan and his old friend and foreign secretary, Lord Home, feared backing Khrushchev into a corner by giving him no alternative except to carry out his ultimatum. Kennedy thought the two sides' positions too far apart to permit a compromise, but decided it would be useful to establish a personal connection with the Soviet leader. "I had been advised on [Khrushchev's] views," he later elucidated in a televised address to the nation. "But . . . it is my duty to make decisions that no adviser and no ally can make for me. It is my obligation and responsibility to see that these decisions are as informed as possible, that they are based on as much direct, firsthand knowledge as possible. I therefore thought it was of immense importance that I know Mr. Khrushchev, that I gain as much insight and understanding as I could on his present and future policies."

Did he think Khrushchev would be restrained by experiencing the resolution of the president?

"I wanted to make certain Mr. Khrushchev knew this country and its policies. I wanted to present our views to him directly, precisely, realistically, and with an opportunity for discussion and clarification."

Kennedy had come into office after the plans had been made to back a group of Cuban exiles seeking by military means the ouster of Fidel Castro. The resulting Bay of Pigs operation was somewhere between a fiasco and a disaster. Kennedy showed a cunning skill in addressing the American people on television and declaring that, as commander in chief, he had to bear the responsibility for the misadventure. Analysts then, and subsequently, did not dispute that the idea of liberation had originated with the Eisenhower administration, or that it was indeed a fiasco. But it was President Kennedy who had denied the expeditionary force critical support from the air, which its officers had been led to believe would be furnished.

The whole thing left the new president wary, and dissatisfied with Allen Dulles's CIA, which, on his reading, had foreseen victory.

At age forty-three, John Kennedy was a generation or more younger than the other major players on the Berlin front, excepting forty-seven-year-old Willy Brandt, mayor of West Berlin. JFK, two generations younger than Adenauer, had no age barrier to worry about. Indeed, he had run against Vice President Richard Nixon, himself only forty-seven, invoking his singular youthful vigor and the need to prod America into motion in search of a New Frontier. He was temperamentally impatient, and his nagging, chronic back trouble was a disincentive to long meetings in the White House tradition. He sharply reduced the frequency of full Cabinet sessions, and he gave all his top aides the same title—Special Assistant—and instructed them to bring important questions directly to him, not to the relevant cabinet member. The American historian Honoré Catudal wrote of the new regime as designed "to replace the pyramid with the wheel, and JFK was to be at the hub."

When news came to Kennedy in February 1961 of Khrushchev's letter to Adenauer, he set up an ad hoc advisory group. To head it, he named the tough, polished Dean Acheson. Quickly the committee became known as the Acheson Review Group, in acknowledgment of the august presence of the former secretary of state. The committee's mandate was to explore every aspect of the Berlin Crisis.

Seared by the experience of the Bay of Pigs, Kennedy reacted to shield himself from a recurrence of what in his judgment had been inadequate briefing by the CIA and the State Department. Accordingly, he resolved to oversee personally the work of the Acheson group, immersing himself so directly in it that State Department officials took to referring to him as "the Berlin desk officer." His close aide Theodore Sorensen described his modus operandi: "[The president] reviewed and revised the military contingency plans, the conventional force build-up, the diplomatic and propaganda initiatives, the Budget changes and the plans for economic warfare. He considered the effect each move would have on Berlin morale, Allied unity, Soviet intransigency and his own legislative and foreign-aid program. He talked to Allied leaders, to Gromyko and to the Germans; he kept track of all the cables; he read transcripts of all the conferences; and he complained (with limited success) about the pace at the Department of State, about leaks from Allied clearances and about the lack of new diplomatic suggestions."

This account would provoke Martin J. Hillenbrand, director of the State Department's Office of German Affairs, to remark that the president might indeed "have done all these things, but there were some surprising gaps in his knowledge." Most importantly, JFK didn't understand to what extent Germans regarded Berlin as a single city and would be appalled at its being severed.

McGeorge Bundy, President Kennedy's national security adviser, had been sharply critical of presidential habits.

After the Bay of Pigs he sent JFK a memo: "Truman and Eisenhower did their daily dozen in foreign affairs the first thing in the morning, and a couple of weeks ago you asked me to begin to meet you on this basis. I have succeeded in catching you on three mornings, for a total of about 8 minutes, and I conclude that this is not really how you like to begin the day. Moreover, 6 of the 8 minutes were given not to what I had for you but what you had for me from Marguerite Higgins, David Lawrence, Scotty Reston, and others. . . .

"Right now it is so hard to get to you with anything not urgent and immediate that about half of the papers and reports you personally ask for are never shown to you because by the time you are available you clearly have lost interest in them." But the president was sharply interested in the Soviet ultimatum.

As secretary of state for President Truman, Acheson had been much criticized when China was taken over by Mao Tse-tung's Communists, and when, nine months later, the North Koreans attacked the South, bringing on a costly war. Acheson's accommodationist policies, it was widely argued, had encouraged these developments. In the decade that followed, Acheson had veered to hard-line anti-Communist policies. He would never flinch again, and he argued now for an unyielding policy against the Soviet Union: (1) Do not negotiate, and (2) be prepared, if the Communists try to isolate Berlin again as they did in 1948, to dispatch an army division down the autobahn from Helmstedt to Berlin.

Administration officials divided, some of them lining up with Acheson, some in favor of negotiation. Walt Rostow, the feisty MIT economist serving as deputy to Mac Bundy, was a hard-liner; so were Allen Dulles, the lame-duck CIA director; Foy Kohler, assistant secretary of state, whose practice of keeping information to himself greatly annoyed Robert Kennedy; and the Joint Chiefs of Staff. Against Acheson's indomitability were ardent New Frontiersmen Arthur Schlesinger Jr., the historian serving as a presidential assistant, and Ted Sorensen. But also seasoned diplomats and men of affairs, including Secretary of State Dean Rusk, who was notoriously cautious, and who had taken a dislike to Germans during a semester spent studying in Berlin in 1934, while Hitler was consolidating his power; Undersecretary of State Chester Bowles, committed Democratic liberal; Averell Harriman, former ambassador to Moscow, serving now as roving ambassador for JFK and laboring to move up in the pecking order; Charles Bohlen, an old Soviet hand, personal translator for FDR at Yalta and Truman at Potsdam, and later Ike's ambassador to Moscow; and State Department legal adviser Abram Chayes, a Harvard-trained lawyer and an old friend of Chester Bowles. Chayes summarized the views of the soft-liners: Acheson's suggestions were "dangerous," likely not to defuse the crisis but to heighten it, indeed "intensifying it to the brink of war."

What loomed was the summit meeting with Khrushchev, to be held in Vienna. The White House wanted nothing in the nature of high expectations for that meeting. Better to think of it as mere diplomatic routine. To that end, it was scheduled so as to make it appear to be merely a way station on JFK's already scheduled state visit to Paris.

In the sober perspective of 1961, summit meetings were not widely regarded as catalysts of peace and freedom. The first four-power summit after Potsdam had been in Geneva in 1955, with the principals being President Eisenhower, Premier Edgar Faure, Premier Nikolai Bulganin, and Prime Minister Anthony Eden. There had been some amusing punctilio having to do with rank. Since President Eisenhower, unlike his opposite numbers, was head of state as well as head of government, he became the chairman of the first day's sessions and delivered the first statement. On the Soviet side, while Khrushchev had held on to his position of first secretary through all the post-Stalin jockeying and was by then the most powerful man in the Kremlin, the actual head of government was Bulganin. And so, while Khrushchev was present as a member of the Soviet delegation, it was Bulganin who spoke officially with the Western leaders.

The summit ended with inconclusive results— predictably, given that the Western leaders' agenda was to achieve German reunification and allow free elections in Eastern Europe, whereas the Soviets' agenda was to create what Bulganin called an "all-European security pact," whose main aim was to remove U.S. forces from Europe.

A successor two-power meeting was held at Camp David in 1959, again with inconclusive results. The atmosphere was cordial, and this cordiality became known as the Spirit of Camp David. But Eisenhower wanted verification procedures for any disarmament agreement, and Khrushchev could not accept that, since it might actually have led to disarmament.

Macmillan and de Gaulle both spent most of 1959 pressing for a new four-power summit.

It finally convened at the Elysée Palace on May 16, 1960, and broke up three hours later. Khrushchev had worked up an uproarious protest of the United States' U-2 surveillance flights over Soviet territory. (Francis Gary Powers had been shot down just two weeks before.) These flights, he raged, were "inadmissible provocative actions." Such surveillance would be justifiable only "when countries are in a state of war." He demanded an outright apology from Eisenhower as the condition for continuing the summit meeting, and he withdrew his invitation for Eisenhower to visit the Soviet Union the next month, explaining with his characteristic heavy irony that the Americans' actions had made it impossible for the USSR "to receive the president with the proper cordiality with which the Soviet people receive welcome guests." De Gaulle tried to deflect Khrushchev's anger by pointing out that a Soviet Sputnik was currently overflying France eighteen times a day, and did that not constitute spying? Absolutely not, said the first secretary: there are no cameras on our Sputnik. How, then, de Gaulle replied, did the Sputnik take pictures of the dark side of the moon? Well, that was a different technology. Finally Khrushchev wondered out loud whether Eisenhower was mentally fit to discharge office. He left the room fuming.

As a follow-up to this performance, Khrushchev decided that he would personally lead the Soviet delegation to the UN General Assembly session that fall. In his 2½-hour opening speech, he again denounced the U-2 flights, and accused the Western powers of destroying "all the foundations of international cooperation." Macmillan obliquely replied to Khrushchev a few days later, suggesting that the great powers should put the failure of the Paris summit behind them and concentrate on moving forward. Khrushchev angrily interrupted him, shouting, "You send your planes over our territory, you are guilty of aggression." Khrushchev was finally gaveled into silence, and Macmillan was able to complete his speech; when the delegates applauded him, Khrushchev pounded his desk in anger.

In preparation for the Vienna summit, President Kennedy talked with everyone he could find, it seemed, who had spent time with Khrushchev. The people he interrogated included Senator Hubert Humphrey, chief spokesman of the liberal wing of the Democratic Party in Congress; Walter Lippmann, the sere columnist, whose word was holy in the deliberative councils of U.S. liberals; James Reston, the No. 1 columnist and news analyst of the *New York Times;* and Soviet savant Chip Bohlen. Kennedy got exhaustive briefing books from the State Department. He studied minutes of Eisenhower's three summits with Khrushchev. He reestablished a speaking relationship with Allen Dulles, from whom he got everything the CIA had accumulated on Khrushchev's quirks. A useful piece of advice from the psychologists retained by the CIA: *Keep your eye on Khrushchev's left temple vein,* to see if he is slipping into a combative mode. Most obviously mistaken advice, from the State Department: Khrushchev was "likely" to deport himself with "reasonable firmness, coupled with a pitch for improved U.S.-Soviet relations." Oddest advice from an old Soviet hand: "Don't be too serious" with Khrushchev, Averell Harriman told Kennedy. "Have some fun, get to know him a little, don't let him rattle you."

On Saturday, June 3, Kennedy arrived in Vienna flush from his exuberant visit to Paris. There he had won the approval of his exacting host, and of the French people. De Gaulle was delighted by the fashionable beauty of Jacqueline Kennedy and impressed by her knowledge of French political history and her fluency in the French language. De Gaulle feigned ignorance of the English language. This was effective except that, from time to time, he would correct his interpreter's translation. But for all that the meeting in Paris was a great social success, Kennedy failed in his diplomatic effort to persuade de Gaulle that France had no need for an independent nuclear force. And he could not budge de Gaulle from his hard line in the matter of the Soviet ultimatum.

Arrived in Vienna, the Kennedys were greeted by thousands of Austrians who ignored the drenching rain to register their enthusiasm for the glamorous young American couple. JFK arrived at the American ambassador's residence just in time to greet Khrushchev, who came over from the Soviet ambassador's residence. Khrushchev had made a leisurely journey from Moscow to Vienna by train, stopping along the way to receive the greetings of his subjects. At prearranged station stops, teenage boys and girls were delegated to give him flowers and presents. The stations themselves were hung with the familiar red banners of Communist countries, but instead of the usual Leninist slogans, these were personalized: "We are all with you, dear

Nikita Sergeyevich"; "Glory to Khrushchev—the unshakable champion of peace"; "Khrushchev equals peace."

The two men were photographed shaking hands on the steps, grinning broadly. The departure was vivid from President Eisenhower's reception of Khrushchev in Washington in 1959—Ike was unsmiling for the photographers, a special strain for the convivial general.

Kennedy and Khrushchev proceeded into the music room, accompanied by chosen aides, and joked a bit—always difficult when different languages are spoken—about the disparity in their ages, moving quickly to substantive matters. Little light ensued, but no divisive heat, until JFK introduced the subject of "miscalculation."

The president had been struck, as a Harvard undergraduate, by the series of "accidents" that had brought on World War I. By August 1914 (as in *The Guns of August*), the British and French to the west, the Germans and Austrians in Central Europe, and the Russians to the east had all mobilized their forces. Incremental mobilizations were perceived by the contending powers as offensive in nature and design. The cordite was in place and ready for any spark, which came when Archduke Franz Ferdinand was assassinated in Sarajevo by a Serbian nationalist, Gavrilo Princip. JFK regularly lectured aides on the point, and now he lectured Khrushchev. The danger in the tense days ahead, he said, was from a spark, especially in Berlin. There, in 344 square miles, was a powder keg, and the explosive dimension of a spark lit there would be thermonuclear. The most important responsibility of world leaders was to keep doused any nascent spark.

Upon reciting his familiar monitory exposition on the

subject of sparks, Kennedy found that he had there and then ignited something of a powder keg. Khrushchev "went berserk," as JFK described the scene to aide Kenny O'Donnell after gratefully concluding the afternoon session. "He started yelling, '*Miscalculation! Miscalculation! Miscalculation!* All I ever hear from your people and your news correspondents and your friends in Europe and everyplace else is that damned word "miscalculation"! You ought to take that word and bury it in cold storage and never use it again! I'm sick of it.'"

The term, Khrushchev said, his voice pitched high, was a "Western" concept, nothing more than "a clever way of making threats." He hammered his point home, though never actually analyzing Kennedy's point about the historical dangers of apparently minor collisions. The talk turned to Berlin and the question of a divided Germany. Khrushchev reaffirmed his ultimatum: *The Soviet Union would sign a peace treaty with East Germany before the end of the year.* If West Germany and its allies wanted to have a say in the terms of it, they could damn well join in the negotiations. Or they would find that any future discussion of Berlin would be conducted not with him, but with Walter Ulbricht. "I want peace," he concluded affably. "But if you want war, that is your problem."

After the second Sunday session, Kennedy flew to London and sought consolation from Macmillan, who was always hearty, even in grim situations. The next evening, JFK flew home. He would learn on his arrival that Khrushchev attended a reception at the Indonesian embassy in Moscow on Monday evening. Khrushchev's exuberance was marked, even by his standards. He sang, danced, and even played the drum. He was thought by a UPI reporter to be celebrating what he deemed a victory over the leader of the Free World.

How so, a victory?

Well, he had said what he intended to do. And President Kennedy had not said what the West would do.

What exactly, concretely, *would* the West do if, by force, Khrushchev pressed for advantages?

JFK did not know. No one knew.

The evening of Tuesday, June 6, Kennedy went on television to give his account of the summit meeting. "I will tell you now that it was a very sober two days. . . ." (He had put it more directly to James Reston, who was there in Vienna: "Roughest thing in my life.") "There was no discourtesy, no loss of tempers, no threats or ultimatums by either side. No advantage or concession was either gained or given. No major decision was either planned or taken; no spectacular progress was either achieved or pretended." So, what was the public to conclude? "At least the chances of a dangerous misjudgment on either side should now be less, and at least the men on whose decisions the peace in part depends have agreed to remain in contact."

On June 10, one week after the beginning of the Vienna summit, Khrushchev made public the memorandum on the Berlin question that he had handed Kennedy on the second day of their meeting. Five days later, Khrushchev took to the airwaves to repeat the old song: "The conclusion of a peace treaty with East Germany must not be delayed any longer."

The Kremlin had given Ulbricht a copy of the JFK memorandum before publishing it. On June 15 Ulbricht held a press conference of his own—saying? The same thing.

A West German reporter attempted to tease out the implications of Ulbricht's reiteration of Khrushchev's ultimatum. Would it mean a halt in the flow of refugees from the East? They were going into West Berlin at the rate, now, of one thousand every day. Would West Berlin's new status as a "free city," the reporter wanted to know, "mean that the state boundary will be erected at the Brandenburg Gate?"

Ulbricht's bizarre reply went largely unremarked, although a few people noted and remembered it. (One such was Colonel Ernest von Pawel of U.S. military intelligence, who would unambiguously predict the wall to his skeptical intelligence and diplomatic colleagues.) What Ulbricht said was: "I understand by your question that there are in West Germany men who wish that we [would] mobilize the construction workers of the GDR in order to build a wall. I don't know of any such intention. The construction workers of our country are principally occupied with home building, and their strength is completely consumed by this task. Nobody has the intention of building a wall." The sentences were impacted with lies. West Germany had no thought of causing Ulbricht to construct a wall, and the East Germans were hardly overworked in building homes for a population yearning for housing; much of the rubble in East Berlin dating from the wartime bombing had not even been cleared. That just to begin with. Ulbricht dreamed at night of building walls.

.   .   .

By the end of June, Acheson had completed a report titled "The Berlin Crisis." It was received by the president, who summoned only the National Security Council and a handful of selected Democratic senators to discuss it.

It is as simple as this, Acheson said in summarizing the report. Berlin may be the ostensible target, but the Kremlin's objective is larger. The immediate test is of the character of the new American president. The president, said Acheson, could yield the Berlin point to Khrushchev, in which event Khrushchev would be back for more in days ahead. Or he could stand firm.

Most specifically, Acheson continued, the United States must stand by the "three essentials," identified by the State Department in 1958 in response to Khrushchev's first Berlin ultimatum. (1) *Maintain an Allied presence in West Berlin, including the military garrisons.* (2) *Insist on continued air and surface access to West Berlin.* (3) *Assure the freedom and security of West Berlin.* However, in Acheson's use of the qualifier "West," a diplomatic concession had already been made. Even the robust Acheson paper ceded East Berlin (and of course also East Germany) to single-power domination by the Soviet Union.

Well then, what did the affirmation that the Western powers had authority over West Berlin imply? What would be done if the fourth party, the Kremlin, thought otherwise, and acted on its own motions?

Acheson weighed deterrent strategies.

We could threaten nuclear war.

We could drop one bomb "somewhere."

We could do less than that, while still remaining firm— "substantially increasing our forces," on a scale large

enough to make plain that "we had irretrievably committed ourselves to the defense of Berlin." We would need to
shore up our troop strength in Germany and also our
nuclear reserves. If then another blockade of Berlin
were imposed, we would need to act decisively—using
conventional forces, but the full might of America would
be manifest.

Acheson's opponents were led by Schlesinger and
Sorensen. The city of Berlin, they insisted, was the sole
objective of the Soviet offensive, not merely a starting
point for grander designs. They quoted Macmillan: The
United States must not back Khrushchev into a corner.
They argued their case fervently, in memos and meetings.
When the battle was over, notwithstanding Acheson's
power as advocate and the brilliance of his exposition, the
soft-liners were in the ascendant.

While in the great power salons arguments were made,
contingency plans considered, and data interpreted, East
Germans were arriving at fateful personal decisions. To go,
or to stay? To leave East Germany meant to leave virtually
everything they owned. There were great human consid-
erations: an aged parent who did not elect to be uprooted;
a divided vote within a two-member family.

Even so, in June 1961, twenty thousand Easterners
went West. On July 6, Ulbricht gave the ambivalents an
added incentive to leave. He unveiled his "Peace Plan of
the German People." There was nothing in the Ulbricht
plan very different from what had been deduced as consequences of Khrushchev's various ultimatums. Still, this

came not from Moscow but from East Berlin, and East Germans saw it as unmistakably clear that Ulbricht was seeking a near-term solution to the Berlin Problem. The Germans had a word for it: Torschluss—shutting the gate. The following day, July 7, East German authorities announced that all Grenzgänger—literally, border-crossers: i.e., East Germans who could not find work, or suitable work, at home and therefore commuted to jobs in West Berlin—would thenceforward be required to register with their local worker unit and solicit permission to continue commuting. Even those who were so licensed could no longer buy "luxury items": no more refrigerators, cars, or washing machines for anyone not employed in the East. The hostility went so far as to deny to the unfortunate wife of a Grenzgänger care in an East Berlin emergency room. The attendants argued that workers who were disloyal to their homeland did not qualify for free medical care in Democratic Germany. The woman, who was hemorrhaging after a miscarriage, died before her husband could get her treated in a Western hospital.

Ulbricht could find yet more screws to tighten. He ordered a drastic reduction in the number of passenger trains going from other East German cities to Berlin. The ubiquitous Volkspolizei (Vopos—the East German police) increased surveillance of autobahns and railroads. Anyone traveling toward Berlin with so much as a small suitcase risked being thrown off the train or required to turn back on the highway.

Refugees seeking Western shelter came up with inventive stories to account for their travel. *We never had time for a honeymoon, and now it's our fifth anniversary. I want my husband to meet my uncle for the first time.* Some sought protection from interrogation by persuading a friend who lived in East Berlin and had a car to pick them up in another East German city—cars with East Berlin license plates were let through the checkpoints; cars from elsewhere in the Soviet Zone were turned back. Once arrived in East Berlin, refugees still faced the challenge of the last leg, into the freedom of West Berlin. Usually they took a chance on the U-bahn (the subway) or the S-bahn (the elevated train), where they banked on blending into the crowd—unlike pedestrians, who were likely to be noticed by border patrols. Families would often travel separately, hoping to avoid suspicion. This—separated families, making their way individually—brought special anguish. Those who got through told their stories at Marienfelde, stories of mounting fears as a daughter or father or wife failed to turn up, stories of desperate pain, or of elated relief when the missing one finally did arrive. Interrogators reported that newcomers were often reluctant to speak of their high-wire adventures. Only after four or five days had gone by did they internalize the sense of security: No one at this refugee camp was going to report what they said to the Vopos, or to the more dreaded Stasi, East Germany's Gestapo. So they spoke out about what they had been through, and what it was they had left behind.

"I've got a terrible problem," Kennedy had told James Reston in Vienna. The influential *New York Times* reporter wasn't permitted in the room when JFK met with Khrushchev, but he spoke with the president immediately after the summit meeting. "If [Khrushchev] thinks I'm inexperienced and have no guts, until we remove those ideas, we won't get anywhere with him. So we have to act." Act how? The question vexed the president and his advisers. On July 17, Ted Sorensen suggested another television address. Explain, Sorensen urged, "our rights, obligations, and objectives" in Berlin, emphasizing "endurance rather than emergency actions." Besides informing the American people, Sorensen reasoned, such an address would advise the Russians "to negotiate before the nuclear stage is reached."

The president spent nearly every summer weekend at the Kennedy compound in Hyannisport. On the weekend of July 22–23 he labored over four drafts, written out on yellow legal pad, of the talk Sorensen recommended. Back in Washington, the draft was reviewed by every New Frontiersman in sight, with Sorensen acting as chief editor. At 9:30 P.M. on July 25, Kennedy walked from his private quarters in the White House to the Oval Office and delivered the heavily worked-over speech.

He seemed uncharacteristically nervous. The sound engineers had required the air conditioner to be turned off, and the president was sweating heavily. But he got through the forty-minute speech with only a couple of flubs.

"We recognize the Soviet Union's historical concern about their security in Central and Eastern Europe, after a series of ravaging invasions, and we believe arrangements can be worked out which will help to meet those concerns." That was conciliatory and touched on a theme the Russians liked to hear, their victimization by Western aggressors.

"We have previously indicated our readiness to remove the actual irritants in West Berlin." Said irritants were not named, and hard-liners such as James O'Donnell, a veteran journalist serving now as assistant to Undersecretary of State George Ball, were left apprehensive: What did the president mean? On the other hand, stern material, of the Dean Acheson school, came quickly. "The world is not deceived by the Communist attempt to label Berlin a hotbed of war. There is peace in Berlin today. The source of world trouble and tension is Moscow, not Berlin. . . . It is the Soviets who have stirred up this crisis. . . . It is they who have opposed free elections. It is they who have rejected an all-German peace treaty, and the rulings of international law. And as Americans know from our history on our own old frontier, gun battles are caused by outlaws, and not by officers of the peace."

The American reaction was reassuring. The public fell into line behind the commander in chief, the Senate approved his plans for a defense buildup in two unanimous roll-call votes, and press reaction was overwhelmingly positive. Again reassuringly, government officials and also opposition leaders praised the speech, in Britain, France, the Netherlands, and Italy. Adenauer sent Kennedy a telegram of thanks, and socialist Willy Brandt, mayor of West Berlin, insisted that approval of Kennedy should be unanimous: "Anyone who bears responsibility and thinks responsibly will be deeply impressed." Brandt was sure that the "Amis"—German slang for "Americans"—would come through if a crisis arose. Only a few Americans were recorded as thinking the speech less than what was required. The U.S. commandant in West Berlin, Major

General Albert Watson, stumbled over the same thing that depressed James O'Donnell: Whenever the president spoke of measures the United States was prepared to take, the word "Berlin" was prefaced by the word "West."

The Communists did not, either in Moscow or in Berlin, appear to dwell on the tacit concession that East Berlin was theirs to deal with as they chose. The official East German daily, *Neues Deutschland,* criticized Kennedy's "warlike tones," which was rhetoric to be expected. TASS, the official Soviet news agency, announced that the president had succumbed to "war fever"—again, Communist boilerplate.

What hadn't been anticipated was the personal reaction of Nikita Khrushchev. John McCloy, who had served as high commissioner of Germany from 1949 to 1952, succeeding General Lucius Clay, served now as Kennedy's adviser on disarmament. He was in Moscow on official disarmament business and received from Khrushchev, vacationing at his dacha in the Crimea, an expansive invitation—McCloy must come down to the Crimea for a good personal visit. On the first day, July 25, Khrushchev and his guest swam together in his private pool and in the Black Sea. The two men were seen walking amicably in the seaside gardens.

The next day, as McCloy put it in his telegram to the president, "the storm broke." If a sovereign German Democratic Republic elected to cut off access to Berlin, Khrushchev shouted, and the Western powers tried to force their way in, war would certainly break out. Such a war would "be thermonuclear." Kindly inform your president, he told McCloy, that the Soviet Union now has the ability to deliver onto U.S. territory a hundred-megaton "superbomb."

Yes, he did calm down, as so often he did. Before sending McCloy back to Moscow, he told him that he was confident Kennedy was too reasonable actually to fight for Berlin. Couldn't the whole business be worked out? They were, after all, sensible people.

McCloy shot a full telegram to the president. JFK called him back to Washington, where everyone waited for Khrushchev's next move.

On July 30, J. William Fulbright, chairman of the Senate Foreign Relations Committee, went on *Issues and Answers* to talk about the likely consequences of, as the interviewer put it, "clos[ing] West Berlin as an escape hatch for refugees." Fulbright treated the question as a kind of civil reform, on the order of how to handle a scarcity of water in a straitened part of the country. He pronounced that the East Germans could, "without violating any treaty," proceed to take this measure. He then egged them on: "I don't understand why the East Germans don't close their border, because I think they have a right to close it."

This time the West Germans came to life. Surely the senator must have been misreported? said Mayor Brandt. Such an analysis of the Berlin problem was otherworldly. It proceeded without any reference to American-British-French authority over the conquered city. More than one West German suggested that Fulbright should come to Berlin himself before prescribing for its future, though one wonders what Senator Fulbright could have been shown that would have altered his analysis. He hadn't spoken as if East Berlin were comfortable enough to cease generating people who wished to flee it. There was nothing in the history of the diplomacy that had created the current status of

Berlin that the learned senator, former professor and sometime university president, couldn't comprehensively examine at the Library of Congress. There was nothing going on in Berlin that would deflect his accommodationist tendencies, which would flower completely five years later when he insisted that the Tonkin Gulf resolution, for which he had voted, had not in fact granted President Johnson authority to combat the refugee problem in another part of the world, containing North Vietnamese pressures against the millions who had fled Hanoi to join the non-Marxist South Vietnamese.

The East German press, understandably, hailed the "realistic opinion" of an enlightened American senator and the "compromise formula" it offered, adding gleefully that Fulbright's statement "has caused great exasperation in Bonn."

In 1960, American spy satellites spotted a new construction site about fifteen miles north of Berlin. The area appeared solidly walled off, and the way in which the rows of excavations were configured suggested that what was being built was a missile-launching site. CIA headquarters in Washington flogged the CIA team in Berlin to find out exactly what was going on. The site was exceptionally well guarded, and CIA Berlin was nearing despair when one of the thousands of refugees at Marienfelde disclosed that he was the architect of the project. From him the CIA learned that it wasn't a missile site at all, it was Walter Ulbricht's present to himself and his Politburo colleagues: a self-contained residential compound near Lake Wandlitz, on the edge of the Bernau forest.

This was no rusticated park, with houses artfully scattered over the grounds. Like Levittown and its imitators in postwar America, the Wandlitz houses were lined up in strict rows (which is what the satellites had observed) and were identical in floor plan. They all had three stories (the third being for servants), a picture window in the living room, beige stucco on the outer walls. Communal amenities included a swimming pool with a retractable glass roof, a banquet hall, tennis courts, a rifle range, and special shops with items not available to ordinary East Germans. The whole thing was surrounded by a double concrete wall about 12 feet high and guarded by 160 carefully selected troops.

Not all of Ulbricht's colleagues were pleased about moving fifteen miles out into the countryside. Erich Mielke, who as minister of state security was chief of the Stasi, did not like being separated so far from his drinking buddies in the Pankow district of Berlin, and he had enjoyed living in Hermann Göring's old house. But Mielke was given no choice, and he found a consolation in the move. The basement of his new house was large enough to permit him his favorite recreation, besides drinking: pistol target shooting. If he could have managed to drink and shoot at the same time, one gathers he'd have been totally content.

While Mielke was installing his target range, other Politburo members found more conventional ways of personalizing their homes. For Otto Grotewohl, who had been a colleague and rival of Ulbricht's ever since the first postwar East German regime, it was expensive carpets and sixteenth- and seventeenth-century furnishings. Erich Honecker was Politburo member for security and head of the Free German Youth, the GDR's version of Moscow's Young Pioneers or the Hitler Jugend. He was a generation younger than Ulbricht and Grotewohl, and his tastes were more modern. He had managed, on his Workers' and Peasants' salary, to acquire an impressive art collection, including a Picasso. Deputy Premier and Minister of Defense Willi Stoph, a former artilleryman, covered his walls with antique swords and firearms. Ulbricht was the most modest and bourgeois of the lot, his taste running to comfortable upholstered sofas and lace doilies on the tables, although he did have Venetian glass mosaics installed in his dining-room floor.

On July 31, East Germany moved another player on the chessboard. With a marvelous discountenance of reality, Herr Ulbricht's Ministry of Health discovered a polio epidemic in West Germany, which had never before been noticed, not even by polio victims. The ministry publicly requested the government to impose strict travel restrictions between East and West Germany, including East and West Berlin, to guard East Germans against polio contamination.

The same day—Polio Day—Ulbricht brought Willi Stoph along on an ultrasecret trip to Moscow. Two weeks earlier, Ulbricht had asked for an emergency meeting of the Warsaw Pact leaders. Khrushchev agreed to such a meeting and scheduled it for August 3. But Ulbricht wanted an earlier opportunity to lobby the Soviet leader about East Germany's distress.

Khrushchev greeted Ulbricht and Stoph warmly but

excused himself from meeting with them then, on the grounds that he had important meetings already scheduled, from which he couldn't pull away. He did think to caution Ulbricht to stay out of sight, as any recognition of him in Moscow might give rise to unwanted speculation. Ulbricht got about in a curtained limousine, and went unnoticed by Western diplomats and reporters.

When the plenary session convened on August 3, Ulbricht, as the first scheduled speaker, was given a disciplinary assignment. He was told to rebuke the Albanian delegation for unruly behavior at a previous Warsaw Pact meeting. After other speakers echoed Ulbricht's rebuke, the Albanians, led by Politburo member Ramiz Alia, stormed out of the chamber. This was exactly as Khrushchev had hoped. The Albanian connection was a bit shaky. The ultraorthodox Enver Hoxha, who had declined to come to Moscow, sending Alia instead, was courting Mao Tse-tung as the supreme Marxist. There hadn't been an open rift, but Khrushchev didn't want a discussion of the super-touchy Berlin question to take place with the Albanians in the room.

Ulbricht wanted two things from his Warsaw Pact colleagues. First, the consummation of the separate peace treaty. Then, their endorsement of comprehensive measures to stop the refugee flow. These would include restrictions on westbound air traffic. Ulbricht didn't want airplanes full of "fascist defectors" lifting off from West Berlin and landing in West Germany. Most importantly, these measures would include a barrier within Berlin itself. Ulbricht revealed that his government already had, dating back to 1952, a definite plan. This had been drawn up in retaliation for diplomatic initiatives between the Allies and West Germany. The plan was officially referred to as the "secret seal-off matter" (geheime Verschlusssache). Western intelligence had got wind of it, and it had become known in the CIA as Operation Chinese Wall. The first stage involved stringing a barbed-wire fence and beefing up security forces all along the twenty-eight-mile-long border. The second stage involved nothing less than building an impregnable concrete wall.

Khrushchev introduced sobering thoughts. Moscow would not, he said, run the risk of interfering with air traffic flying out of the three airfields in West Berlin. Khrushchev the Cautious went a disconcerting step further. Yes, he had said he would conclude a separate peace treaty, but there was no reason to be precipitate. There was division in the ranks of the Western leaders. Nothing would be lost by putting off the signing of the new treaty until the Western powers had arrived at a position that might edge in the direction of conciliation. Differences among the Allies could be exploited in the course of negotiating a new free-city status for West Berlin.

But all of this was said in the context of Ulbricht's plans to close the city. What precautions would Comrade Ulbricht take to guard against the division of Berlin issuing in such an uprising as that of June 17, 1953, which had so shaken East Germany? And what exactly would Ulbricht do if the action Adenauer had been urging on the Allies were then to take place: a total economic boycott of East Germany?

Ulbricht and Stoph left Moscow immediately after that session and made their stealthy way home, landing at Schönefeld Airfield shortly after midnight. From there they went directly to Wandlitz. Arrived at his house, Ulbricht found, waiting, three of his most trusted deputies: Erich Honecker; Erich Mielke; and Bruno Leuschner, the chairman of the State Planning Commission.

Ulbricht briefed them on the deliberations in Moscow and handed out assignments. Stoph, Mielke, and Honecker were to report on just how many East German troops could be deployed to prevent a general revolt, or to put it down if it eventuated. Leuschner was to consider the effects on the country's economy if Adenauer succeeded in halting shipments of chemicals, high-grade steel, and specialized machinery. Both reports, Ulbricht ordained, would be brought to him by 10:00 A.M. That was a mere matter of hours away.

He explained that he needed this information first in order to share it with chosen members of the GDR Politburo. He would then return to Moscow and use it in a presentation at the last session of the Warsaw Pact meeting.

A logistical question was: Where would Ulbricht meet with his Politburo colleagues? Distracting rumors were already circulating: Where was Ulbricht? He had missed an impromptu reception for Ghanian president Kwame Nkrumah, who had unexpectedly turned up in Berlin. If Ulbricht then called a meeting with leading Politburo members, whether at his home in Wandlitz or at Central Committee headquarters near Unter den Linden, people would wonder what was going on. Surely he would not have deliberately snubbed the pro-Communist black leader of Ghana? He must have been attending to grave matters of state. Like what?

With what in any other man would have looked like a

bout of defiant humor, Ulbricht settled on an explanation for it all. He had been called by the Ministry of Health to discuss the polio epidemic in West Germany!

The meeting at the Ministry of Health that Friday morning did not open with a discussion of polio. The first question was: What supplies needed by East Germany would not be available in the event of a Western boycott?

Leuschner was reassuring. There was nothing, he stated confidently, the GDR might need that couldn't be supplied by other Warsaw Pact nations. A Western embargo could be shrugged off.

Stoph's report introduced complications. Local forces in Berlin couldn't simultaneously set about sealing off West Berlin and also keep order. Militiamen from outside Berlin would need to be brought in.

Very well. That, Ulbricht said, could be done, and Honecker's Free German Youth could be mobilized to help out.

Most important, East Germany now had at its disposal the Volksarmee, the People's Army. At the time of the 1953 uprising, a true GDR army hadn't existed, and Ulbricht had had no alternative but to cry out for help to the Red Army. Now an East German army did exist, and it was a disciplined force purged of unreliable ideological elements. It was quite up to the job, said Stoph, of suppressing any new uprising.

The question now was: timing.

It would not do to provoke a major dislocation. The inner Iron Curtain could not be installed while the Grenzgänger, the East German commuters, were at work in West Berlin, or in transit

So it had to be done at night. And, better, on a weekend night. This made sense even putting the Grenzgänger to one side. The enemy is assumed to be somnolent on weekends.

Yes, and the enemy's General Bruce Clarke, U.S. Army commander in Europe, had meditated on the same point. Earlier in the week he had told his subordinates: "Pearl Harbor came on Sunday morning, North Korea attacked South Korea on Sunday morning. . . ." So General Clarke imposed a strict curfew on all GIs based in West Germany who were not officially on leave.

Ulbricht and Stoph once again boarded their jet plane for their second three-hour flight in twenty-four hours.

The Warsaw Pact leaders received Ulbricht's reassurances and seemed satisfied with them. But there was still the question of what exactly the West might do, thus pressed.

Khrushchev eventually came up with the compromise formula:

- Ulbricht should order his troops, at Hour X, to begin stringing the barbed wire.
- But if the Allies responded with force, the GDR troops were to drop back.

Don't be apprehensive on the point, he reassured Ulbricht. Consider President Kennedy's speech on July 25, in which he warned only against an assault on *West* Berlin. Consider Senator Fulbright's comments, in which he simply deferred to the authority of the GDR. Still, Khrushchev would put Soviet troops on alert. To underscore his commitment to the GDR, he called into the room Marshal Ivan S. Koniev, World War II hero, second in command in the Soviet conquest of Berlin. Khrushchev announced that he was sending Koniev to Berlin to act as commander in chief of the Soviet forces in East Germany.

The rest was just tidying up. A cover story was needed to feed to the foreign intelligence services, which would be wondering what exactly was going on behind the Kremlin walls.

The resulting communiqué announced that the Warsaw Pact states had met to reaffirm their demand for a peace treaty with both German states before the end of the year. This was sleeping-pill time. The announcement was scantily treated in the press.

Ever since 1945, Berlin had been the spy capital of the Cold War. Neutral Vienna was important, too, as a place where both the KGB and the OSS/CIA could operate freely, but the agents on both sides had a harder edge in Berlin. As soon as the Americans were permitted into the city (held initially only by the Soviets) in July 1945, Allen Dulles moved his OSS European operations center there from Bern, Switzerland. For the U.S. mission he chose a house in Dahlem, a tree-lined neighborhood in the southwestern part of the city that had been spared heavy bomb damage. At the same time, the Soviets were converting for use as their headquarters a German combat training school in Karlshorst, a less fashionable but still comfortable, and also undamaged, quarter in the southeastern part of the city. The Soviets' base, however, was far larger than the Americans', and became their military as well as intelligence headquarters in Germany.

The OSS also had intended to make Berlin its German headquarters. It soon became apparent, though, that the peculiar conditions in a divided city, and the fact that the American military's headquarters could not be closer than Frankfurt, halfway across the American Zone, meant that the OSS/CIA outpost in Berlin would have to be an operations base, not a full-fledged station.

That did not in any sense make it a backwater. Most of the men who became CIA station chiefs in the Sixties and Seventies had done a stint in Berlin in the Fifties or Sixties. There was a Wild West atmosphere there, as the KGB regularly crossed over into West Berlin to kidnap or kill, and the CIA (as it formally became in 1947) cultivated locals to bring back information, often at great risk, from behind enemy lines.

The chief of Berlin Operations Base (BOB) from 1953 to 1959 was Bill Harvey, a former FBI man who always carried a pistol. His most famous undertaking was Operation Gold, which entailed tunneling under the border to tap into the East German telephone system. The idea was that, given the importance of Karlshorst to the Soviets' East European operations, most critical communications in that theater would go through the East Berlin switches. Tap them, and we would have an unparalleled source of knowledge of Soviet intentions.

Operation Gold ultimately failed, betrayed by British double agent George Blake. But it survived in the lore of occupied Berlin.

. . .

On Monday, August 7, Khrushchev was back on television to give what had been advertised as a major foreign-policy address. It was substantially a public reiteration of what he had boasted to John McCloy in the Crimea. The Soviet Union, he said, now had enough weapons to destroy American military bases everywhere in the world. The Russians had, moreover, a "superbomb" so mighty that it could turn Germany into "dust." Soviet technology was triumphant. Earlier in the day, Khrushchev reported, cosmonaut Gherman S. Titov had landed safely after orbiting the earth seventeen times in twenty-five hours. Khrushchev reiterated his call for Great Britain, France, and the United States to join the Soviet Union at a round-table conference.

On August 9, the Berlin Watch Committee held its regular Wednesday afternoon meeting. This was the high-guard U.S. team—military intelligence, CIA, and State Department. On this particular Wednesday, the CIA was represented by the deputy chief of BOB, John Dimmer. The former chief of base, David Murphy, had just rotated back to CIA headquarters in Washington, D.C. (the grand compound in Langley was not yet completed), and the new chief, William Graver, was too busy settling in to attend the pro forma meeting.

Both Colonel Ernest von Pawel and Colonel Thomas McCord of military intelligence told their colleagues that something dramatic was going to happen soon, and that the likeliest development was a barrier along the border dividing East from West Berlin. Von Pawel emphasized the internal logic of the Berlin situation: sealing the outside perimeter of the whole city would not prevent the East-to-West hemorrhage. Nor should it be forgotten that the Germans had experience in dividing cities with walls. A wall had been built in Warsaw twenty-one years earlier, designed to seal in the Jewish ghetto.

Von Pawel and McCord's colleagues on the Watch Committee didn't deny that *something* was imminent, but they were certain it would not be a wall. As Dimmer put it, Ulbricht would be committing "political suicide" if he built such a wall.

As the Watch Committee met, Moscow celebrated its cosmonauts, Titov and his predecessor in space, Yuri Gagarin, in a two-hour-long parade on Red Square. That evening, at a huge reception in St. George's Hall in the Kremlin, Khrushchev raised his champagne glass and addressed the assembly of diplomats, scientists, and engineers. He turned to the theme of war. "We never bowed when the Germans came close to Moscow and Leningrad," he declaimed. "Do you think we will bow down now because of Adenauer? If Adenauer with his Bundeswehr thinks he can achieve reunification through war and we are attacked, then there will be no German nation left. All Germany will be reduced"—once again—"to dust. We are not threatening anybody, but we are not going to tremble like cowards."

At 10:00 A.M. on Friday, August 11, the Volkskammer—the East German parliament—was called to order. Outside, the posters rang out: "Give Us More Protection Against Bonn's Headhunters"; "Protect Our Republic against the Slave Traders!" Adam Kellett-Long, the young East Berlin correspondent for Reuters, was accustomed to

Communist rhetoric, but the resolutions now passed by the Volkskammer seemed to him to be of a different order. Putting them together with the Torschlusspanik (fear that the gate would be shut) that he found all around him in East Berlin, and remembering Ulbricht's strange statement of June 15, he wrote a long dispatch predicting imminent action. Perhaps the Ulbricht regime would seal off the whole city from the rest of the Soviet Zone; perhaps it would divide the city itself.

Even by Communist standards, Erich Honecker's security for the secret seal-off matter was remarkably thorough. There were virtually no intelligence leaks, and no detailed ones. Alert observers such as von Pawel and Kellett-Long proceeded only by making deductions. Honecker had kept knowledge of the great scope of the operation limited to twenty people. Moreover, his deputies did not report to their ad hoc operations cockpit, on the third floor of East Berlin police headquarters, until 8:00 P.M. on Saturday, when bystanders were few, and unlikely to notice the cadre coming in.

At midnight exactly, Honecker instructed the minister of transportation to halt all U-bahn and S-bahn trains between East and West Berlin. The minister's deputies knew what to do. In 1952, when the seal-off plans were originally drawn up, the switches had been reconfigured to permit reversing the train engines.

Back on Friday, Kellett-Long's Reuters editors had sent out his alarming dispatch, but they almost immediately regretted doing so: surely the young correspondent had been affected by the refugees' panic? On Saturday afternoon, nothing having happened to justify his predictions, Kellett-Long was told to find a way to back down. That evening, he drove around the quiet streets of the Soviet Sector looking for signs of unusual activity. He detected none. Still unshaken from his pessimism, he drove back to his office, northeast of Unter den Linden, and wrestled with his assignment. Just after midnight, the telephone rang. The caller did not introduce himself, and Kellett-Long did not recognize the voice. The caller spoke, in German, a single sentence: "A small suggestion—don't go to bed tonight." Kellett-Long returned to his car and drove toward the Brandenburg Gate. A Vopo stopped him: "The road is closed." He offered no explanation. Kellett-Long drove then to Leipzigerstrasse, intending to continue to Potsdamerplatz. This time a soldier stopped him: "The border is closed."

Kellett-Long drove at maximum speed back to his office and shot off a dispatch to London. At his typewriter, he began to document what he had seen. At 0111 the East German news agency's ticker suddenly started up. It was tapping out a statement from the Warsaw Pact governments. The ticker explained that the Western powers' obstinacy in refusing to negotiate a peace treaty had made it imperative to introduce "reliable supervision and real control" over the East–West boundary.

At 0200 the ticker spat out an official decree of the East German Council of Ministers. The border was now closed.

It was only a few insomniacs, night owls, and Western Sector border guards who saw with their own eyes this turning point in the Cold War taking place. As the rest of the city slept, East German soldiers, militiamen, and police fanned out along the whole twenty-eight miles of the jagged inter-sector border and began stringing barbed wire. It was there in copious supply—Honecker had been stockpiling it in army and militia garrisons since March, when Ulbricht gave him the order. Militiamen with jack-hammers and crowbars began to tear up the paving stones on major streets, making them impassable by ordinary vehicles. Others stood by with tommy guns to block any interference. On the Western side, nightclub patrons, spilling out onto the streets, yelled insults at the Eastern-ers. Some called out, "Wait till the Amis get here!" But the Amis with their tanks, which would have rolled right over the barbed wire, never came.

The CIA's eyes and ears in Berlin started straggling into base just after 0500. It took them four hours after that to get off a telegram to the State Department. The East Ger-mans, it said, were "cutting off movement into West Berlin." That message, received at about 0400 East Coast time, contained a code word indicating that the president should be informed immediately. Even so, it was past 1100 when the duty officer onshore at Hyannisport radioed to the Secret Service man on board the *Marlin*. JFK was tak-ing his father's cabin cruiser to the spot designated for a Sunday picnic. The Secret Service officer was told to inform the president that he had to return to shore for an urgent message.

Kennedy's first reaction was anger at the officials who had failed to keep him informed. On the phone to Dean

Rusk, he demanded, "What the hell is this? How long have you known this? Was there any warning in the last two or three days?" Later, remembering Operation Gold, he asked various subordinates, "Don't we have a tunnel in Berlin?"

The performance by the CIA, the State Department, and the White House staff certainly had not been sterling. Apart from the failure of Berlin Base to take seriously the signs that two military-intelligence officers, a young Reuters reporter, and thousands of East Berliners could clearly see, and apart from the four-hour delay (once Berlin Base was awake) in notifying Washington, and Washington's seven-hour delay in notifying the president, there was total disarray in the State Department. Most of the Berlin Task Force was off on vacation; the ones who were in town seemed paralyzed.

A West German television journalist, Lothar Loewe, turned up at the State Department to find out what his friends there knew. Nothing much, they said. Hadn't they phoned Berlin? he asked. No, they hadn't—they weren't allowed to, because there were no secure phone lines across East Germany. Whereupon Loewe rousted out his friend James O'Donnell. Together they put through a call to a USIA pal in Berlin, from whom they received an up-to-the-minute account of "the intensity of the excitement and distress, the many soldiers, tanks and troop carriers on the line, and the anger of the people." It was from O'Donnell and Loewe that the State Department got its first solid information.

In fact, it would have made very little difference if the president had learned the news at 9:00 P.M. Saturday.

Whether they realized it or not, he and his task force had made their decision a month before: East Berlin was in the Soviets' sphere of influence; the Allies' interest was in West Berlin. That sunny Sunday morning, once Kennedy had spoken with Rusk and been told that the Communists had made no move either to invade West Berlin or to cut off Western access, he calmed down. "Go to the ball game as you had planned," he told his secretary of state. "I am going sailing."

On the seventh floor of the State Department, Foy Kohler put the administration's spin on the seal-off: "After all, the East Germans have done us a favor. That refugee flow was becoming embarrassing." It was clear that Washington was not going to choose this time and place to pay any price, bear any burden.

2

The Continuing Crisis

Later that afternoon, Kohler was on the phone, Secretary Rusk listening in on an extension line. The call was to Allan Lightner, the top-ranking American civilian in Berlin. Lightner was a career diplomat, but less cautious than many of his confreres. He told Kohler that he and the U.S. commandant in Berlin had spent the whole day collaborating with their French and British counterparts. They had come up with what Lightner would later call a "resounding tripartite statement," which they were prepared to release to the press. Kohler, alarmed, put down the phone and consulted with Rusk. When Kohler returned to the phone, he instructed Lightner firmly: Neither he nor his colleagues "were to issue any statement whatsoever." What needed to be said, and how it was said, would be for Washington, D.C., to decide.

Washington came through late in the afternoon. The border closing was not a defeat for the West, the official statement said. It was, in fact, a moral victory. What the world had been given was a vivid demonstration of "the failure of Communism in East Germany." Granted, the border closing violated the Four-Power Agreements worked out by the European Advisory Commission in 1945, which asserted free movement throughout the occupied city. "These violations of existing agreements," the statement limped on, "will be the subject of vigorous protest through appropriate channels." However, the violations were aimed only at the GDR's own people, "and not at the Allied position in West Berlin, nor access thereto." If that were to happen—a genuine challenge to West Berlin— vigorous reaction by the Allies would be expected.

Relief was in the air. De Gaulle was spending the weekend at Colombey-les-Deux-Eglises, and Macmillan was shooting grouse in Yorkshire. Neither statesman publicly or privately sought to challenge the démarche in Berlin, as played out on August 13.

It was not so with the mayor of West Berlin, Willy Brandt. He too was out of town when the border was closed. The West German elections were just a month away, and Brandt was the top figure in the Social Democratic Party, running hard to unseat the aged Adenauer. In the first two weeks of August, Brandt had spent only two days in the city he served as mayor. The rest of the time he was touring the Federal Republic, campaigning.

On Saturday, August 12, he spent the whole day at meetings in Nuremberg, fifteen years after the hanging there of the senior Nazis. The day ended with a huge outdoor rally at the Hauptmarkt, complete with music and fireworks. From there, he and his entourage boarded their private sleeping cars, attached to the Munich–Kiel express. They were headed for the northwestern peninsula of Germany, just south of Denmark.

Brandt was not known for temperance in any sense of the word, and after a day of harsh speeches against the Adenauer government, he and his friends spent a "frolicsome" (ausgelassen) evening, as Brandt would later record, unwinding on the choo-choo. So when a railway official at Hanover barged into his cabin at 4:00 A.M., it took some moments for the news to penetrate: Ulbricht had divided the city. Brandt broke the news to the others, left the train, and phoned his office for details. He and his friends took the first plane from Hanover to Tempelhof Airport, and were driven to Potsdamerplatz.

This had once been the Times Square or Piccadilly Circus of Berlin, but World War II had left it a field of desolation, tram lines torn up, buildings in semi-ruins. And since the border between the American and Soviet Sectors bifurcated it, it had not been high on West Berlin's rebuilding plan. Now it was filled with Vopos using pneumatic drills to tear up the pavement.

"Now look here!" Brandt shouted over the noise of the drilling. *"What is the meaning of this?"* The Vopos went on with their work as if no one was addressing them, let alone the mayor of half of the city in which they were working. "Furchtbar!" he muttered to no one in particular. "Entsetzlich! Schrecklich!" (Dreadful! Atrocious! Terrible!) He stopped by City Hall and went from there to the Kommandantur, the headquarters of the Allied governing body, located in Dahlem, near the CIA's Berlin Base. There he received an attentive hearing, but not much practical help. The British and French generals, Rohan Delacombe and Jean Lacomme, were under the same orders from home as Albert Watson, the American general: *Take*

no action on your own. Watson spoke to Brandt on behalf of the three commandants: "Our respective capitals have been informed. Our governments will make the necessary decisions." Brandt correctly interpreted the generals' message: Nothing, by way of forceful resistance, was authorized. He fired a forlorn parting shot: "The entire East will laugh, from Pankow to Vladivostok."

Twenty miles east of the Kennedys' Hyannisport compound, in the old-line Cape Cod town of Chatham, Marguerite Higgins picked up the telephone and called James O'Donnell in Washington. Higgins had begun her fabled career as a war correspondent at the end of World War II, going deep into Austria with the Seventh Army. As soon as the war ended, she became the *New York Herald Tribune*'s Berlin bureau chief, at age twenty-four. In 1948 she moved on to Tokyo. She was one of the first reporters to enter South Korea after the invasion from the North in 1950. She later married General William Hall, who in early postwar Berlin had been air intelligence officer for General Clay, the military governor. They had all been friends with O'Donnell in Berlin. Higgins now told O'Donnell that Clay, whose summer house was right down the road from hers, shared their misgivings about the "appeasers" in the State Department. She thought there just might be a role for him in Berlin, 1961. Did O'Donnell think she should broach the subject with Clay?

He did.

Twenty minutes later she called O'Donnell back, and Clay was in the room with her. The general had been thinking along much the same lines as Higgins, and wanted to offer his services to the president as a special envoy to Berlin. O'Donnell cautioned him: There would most likely be resentments among standing U.S. military authorities. Even so, he thought it worthwhile to put the proposal before the administration.

Higgins duly called another old friend of hers, Bobby Kennedy, who promised to put the idea up to his brother. There was some back-and-forth over details. Some of JFK's men didn't like the idea of sending a Republican as the president's special representative, and Clay didn't like the initial suggestion that he report to Bobby Kennedy. "I'm a president's man," he told O'Donnell, "but I cannot abide that little brother of his."

But JFK quickly decided that Clay was the man he wanted in Berlin. It didn't escape his notice that, in the long view of it, Clay could be thought responsible for the current Berlin crisis. If it hadn't been for Clay, there wouldn't have been a Free Berlin in 1961 for Ulbricht and Khrushchev to seal off and for the Allies to worry about.

In June 1948, when Stalin decided to end the Berlin problem by starving out West Berlin, the Truman administration, along with the governments of Clement Attlee in London and Robert Schuman in Paris, reacted as Stalin expected. There was no way to resist the Soviet démarche, they concluded, given that, with its current food stocks, West Berlin could not survive for much more than a month. It was Clay who passionately challenged this fatalism. He telexed to the Pentagon: "We have lost Czechoslovakia. Norway is threatened. When Berlin falls, western Germany will be next. If we mean . . . to hold Europe against Communism, we must not budge."

Clay had risen to eminence in the U.S. Army not by charisma, in the fashion of Patton or MacArthur. His wizardry had been logistics. In the fall of 1944, months after D-Day, American efforts to advance against the Germans were hampered by a supply logjam at Cherbourg. Ike dispatched Clay there. In two days, supplies were moving again. In June 1948, Clay swiftly worked out a response to the Communists' blockade: a massive airlift. Soviet soldiers could block surface transport easily, but shooting down U.S. planes would have been an act of war. It was unlikely that Stalin would go so far. Clay arranged for the diversion of all available transport planes to the ends of the airlift. On June 25, the second day of the blockade, the first load of food arrived in Berlin. West Berliners had a rough few months, but the city dug in. In May 1949, Stalin gave up.

The current crisis, twelve years after the blockade, was one more round in the Berlin story. Khrushchev had complained, in his eight-hour conversation with Senator Hubert Humphrey in December 1958, that West Berlin was a "bone in my throat." He was now attempting what Stalin had failed to accomplish.

The formal appointment of Lucius Clay as President Kennedy's personal representative, with the rank of ambassador, wasn't made until August 30, and Clay didn't take up his post officially until September 19. But on Friday, August 18, he flew to Berlin with Vice President Lyndon Johnson on a special mission to show the flag. Johnson hadn't wanted to go. An American military convoy was being sent from West Germany to West Berlin that same weekend. "There'll be a lot of shooting," LBJ protested, "and I'll be in the middle of it. Why me?" But once he was there, his political blood flowed. As his car made its way through the streets of Berlin on the Saturday afternoon, a mere six days after the border closing, he responded to the cheering crowd as if to American voters, getting down from the car to hug women, kiss babies, and pet dogs.

Suddenly the crowd spotted the occupant of the second car in the motorcade. Clay had put on a little weight since he left Berlin in 1949, and his temples had grayed, but the aquiline nose and black eyebrows were instantly recognizable. The shout went up: "Der Clay, der Clay ist hier!" Johnson took it all in, and made one of his on-the-spot decisions: The roaring crowd was more important than picking up speed to reach Potsdamerplatz as planned. All he could do there, after all, was view the nascent wall. He ordered the motorcade to continue in its stately pace back to City Hall, where speeches were made.

The next day was Sunday, but part of Johnson's agenda was to bring back some of the famous German porcelain and high-quality shoes. When Mayor Brandt explained to him that the showrooms and shops were closed, LBJ demanded that they be opened specially for him. At some cost to the mayor's and the merchants' sense of decorum, they were, and he ordered Texas-sized quantities of merchandise.

That evening, he hosted a fried-chicken dinner at the Hilton's rooftop restaurant. As he waved a drumstick over his head, a member of the party, unaccustomed to the ways of LBJ, asked a Secret Service agent, "He's not high, by any chance?"

But the vice presidential visit had done its work, restoring to West Berlin what Edward R. Murrow—who by extraordinary good luck had arrived in Berlin on August 12, on U.S. Information Agency business—described as "that perishable commodity called hope."

For the first few days after August 13, the border remained highly porous, and some of the early escapes had an almost lighthearted air about them. Patrick Habans, a twenty-year-old photographer for *Paris-Match,* had been dispatched to Berlin from Paris on the morning of the 13th, as soon as his editors learned the dramatic news. Habans had never been to Berlin before, and, attempting to make his way to his hotel from Tegel Airport in the French Sector, he got lost, blundering to the border at Lennéstrasse. And there he spotted a photojournalist's dream.

A young couple was embracing, the girl's back up against the Communist side of the brand-new chicken-wire fence. But her young man's attention was not entirely on her: he was industriously using a pair of wire cutters behind her back, their bodies shielding his activity from observers on the eastern side. As Habans clicked his shutter, the young man cut the marginal strand. He whistled, and from the surrounding shrubbery came scores of people. Dozens got themselves through the gap before Vopos arrived, dispersing the crowd and repairing the fence.

A singular case was that of a nineteen-year-old Grepo (short for Grenzpolizei, or border policeman) named

Conrad Schumann. A poor shepherd from Saxony, he had been happy to join the GDR's armed forces to find financial security and, as he later told Western interviewers, to defend his country against "Western military aggressors." He had not expected to find himself in the middle of Berlin, separated by only a few strands of barbed wire from fellow Germans who were yelling, "Pigs! Traitors! Concentration camp guards!" Another, more organized group of demonstrators chanted "Freiheit!" (Freedom!), awakening latent thoughts in Schumann. On his side of the border he saw trucks pulling up and soldiers unloading slabs of concrete. If he didn't bolt now, he might never have another chance. Conrad prayed that his Vopo comrades would obey the orders they had been given—not to shoot into West Berlin. He waited till the nearest Vopos were looking the other way and then clambered across the wire. West German photographer Klaus Lehnartz, lounging against a building on the other side of Bernauerstrasse, captured the moment when Schumann's right boot touched down on the top strand of wire: one of the emblematic photographs of the Cold War.

Bernauerstrasse, a curving residential street a mile or so north of Unter den Linden, had been merely a curiosity; now it became a focal point of the Cold War. When modern Berlin was created by the Weimar government in 1920, the border between the working-class borough of Wedding and the borough of Mitte, the city's administrative center, ran right down the middle of Bernauerstrasse. In 1938 the street sweepers of Wedding complained about the irritating arrangements. The authorities took time out from tending to Der Führer's needs and decreed that the entire street, including both sidewalks (but not including the houses on the southeast side), would now belong to Wedding. When in 1945 the city was carved up into occupation sectors, Mitte—including the houses on the southeast side of Bernauerstrasse—wound up in the Soviet Sector; Wedding—including the space between the two rows of buildings—wound up in the French Sector.

Even under Ulbricht, this had not mattered much—until August 13, 1961. Suddenly residents on the southeast side of the street were ordered to surrender their front-door keys to the Vopos, and the doors were bolted. Windows, however, were still available. Some people jumped impetuously, and were severely injured or even killed. Quickly, the West Berlin authorities sent firemen with nets, permitting many people to jump to safety.

Through much of the center of Berlin, the border followed the Spree River or one of the canals branching off it. Industrial engineer Georg Maurer had thought that he and his wife, Carola, might manage just to walk across one of the bridges over the Teltow Canal, pushing their little daughter in her baby carriage. But all the bridges proved to be blocked. Still, this was one of the many parts of Berlin given over to gardens, which screened the water's edge from the guards' view. The Maurers decided to swim across. As they hunted for a starting point, a gardener took pity and led them to an especially sheltered section. They started swimming. Georg, burdened with the baby, found himself splashing noisily and feared he would attract the attention of the Vopos. But either they did not hear, or they chose not to notice. On the opposite bank, West Berliners did hear, and see. The Maurers were pulled out of the water by welcomers and taken to a West Berlin patrol car, which conveyed them safely to Marienfelde.

One unidentified East Berliner that day was not so lucky. As a crowd of West Berliners, apprehensive, watched him start his run for the border, the Vopos shot him down, yards from the fence at Bethaniendamm.

The porosity of the border was partly a matter of logistics. Even with Honecker's superb superintendence, an impenetrable wall could not be constructed in one night. But it wasn't only logistics. When Khrushchev told Ulbricht on July 31 that he had other urgent meetings to attend, he was not entirely neglecting Berlin. One of the meetings was with Mikhail Menshikov, his ambassador to Washington, and Andrei Smirnov, his ambassador to Bonn. He wanted their thoughts on the Allies' reaction to whatever Ulbricht might propose. Both ambassadors assured him that the Allies would talk tough and do nothing. Menshikov cited the television appearances of Kennedy and Fulbright. Smirnov pointed out that even so nonmilitary a reprisal as a trade embargo wouldn't work: Adenauer had been urging this ever since Khrushchev's February ultimatum, but it threatened too many commercial interests to get sustained backing from his own countrymen or from the Allies.

These reassurances were what permitted Khrushchev to give Ulbricht, at the Warsaw Pact meeting, the conditional authority to proceed. Richard Boehm, a political officer on

Lightner's staff, later wrote, "The Soviets proceeded very cautiously and piecemeal, or at least one step at a time, as if [prepared] to pull in their horns, which they almost invariably did on those rare occasions when Washington stood up, or when we in Berlin took actions on our own initiative." West Berlin's senator of the interior, Joachim Lipschitz, agreed. He urged the Allies to send a few tanks to knock down the barbed wire. When, by Tuesday, they had not done so, Ulbricht concluded that it was safe to proceed with Operation Chinese Wall. Working a few feet back from Sunday's barbed wire, Honecker's men used bricks, cement blocks, concrete slabs, and pressed rubble to start building a more substantial barrier.

By Thursday the 17th, many sections of the border had a wall a yard high; that morning, an assortment of Vopos and militiamen started extending the wall right across Potsdamerplatz. On Bernauerstrasse they bricked up ground-floor windows and ordered residents to leave their apartment doors unlocked, so that Vopos could enter and inspect at any time. Anti-tank barriers—which looked like heavy sawhorses without hind legs—were placed at close intervals across major roads. Honecker was frequently at the border, visibly pleased by the progress and urging the workers on.

This was Ulbricht's hour. On one visit to Potsdamerplatz, he was told by a Volksarmee officer that an American general had recently walked by. The secretary-general replied pompously: "Then he saw that the National People's Army stands at its post and that everything is in order." That was the victorious theme. The official East German newspaper, *Neues Deutschland,* brought to mind the smug self-satisfaction of Hitler in his own early, victorious days. "If peace is endangered, Walter Ulbricht does not hesitate. He restores order by closing the door to further provocations on the part of the warmongers and the war-city hyenas."

Konrad Adenauer's first impulse was to go to Berlin and encourage the free Germans to defy the Communists. But, sitting in Rhöndorf on Sunday and hearing the unfolding story, he agonized over what he should do. Although temperamentally a hard-liner, he shared the fear of the Kennedy administration: that the wrong kind of response by the West would lead to an uprising that in turn would lead to a bloodbath. Would his appearance in Berlin advance or damage the cause of freedom? U.S. senator Thomas Dodd, who had been a prosecutor at the Nuremberg trials, was visiting Adenauer. A defiant anti-Communist, he urged his host to go to Berlin. No, said Adenauer, he must at the very least consult his foreign minister and then the ambassadors of the Allied countries.

Der Alte had still not made his decision when word got to him of what Willy Brandt had said the day before in his Nuremberg campaign speech. The account given to Adenauer quoted Brandt as saying, among other things, that the Christian Democratic Union/Christian Social Union (CDU/CSU) government "exhausts itself in idolatry and haughtiness, and takes refuge in lazy-mindedness and stupidity."

That tipped the scale. Adenauer would proceed on Monday as scheduled to Regensburg, near Nuremberg, for a campaign speech of his own. In that speech, the Old Man skillfully wove in references to the events of the past forty-eight hours, advocated immediate economic sanctions, and turned then to his opponent. After a few minutes of dignified rebuttals of Brandt's attacks, he made a dirty crack. If anybody has been dealt with indulgently during the campaign, he said, "it is Herr Brandt, alias Frahm." This reference to Brandt's bastard birth was lustily applauded by Adenauer's listeners, and if it was meant to get under the mayor's skin, it succeeded. Brandt was in West Berlin planning a mass demonstration for that Wednesday. When told what Adenauer had said, he had to leave the room to compose himself.

Adenauer finally visited Berlin the following week. The crowds were thin, and many people carried placards saying, "At last!" or "It's about time!" Three weeks later, the election returns confirmed that he had made a serious mistake in failing to support Brandt as the West's man on the front line. Adenauer's CDU/CSU coalition, which had always walked away with a majority of the popular vote, dipped below 50 percent. Brandt's Social Democrats (SPD) took 36.3 percent, their highest figure ever.

On August 22, the Ulbricht government issued three new decrees: (1) West Berliners could no longer enter East Berlin simply by showing a valid identity card; they would now have to obtain a special permit. (2) The number of crossing points was reduced from twelve to seven. (3) All inhabitants of West Berlin were to stay one hundred meters back from their side of the border.

This was too much for the Allied commandants. They did not wait for permission from Washington, London, and Paris. They issued a joint communiqué condemning the decrees as illegal. Special offense was taken over the third decree. Here Ulbricht was presuming to make law for Free Berlin. The decrees were "further proof that the East German Communist regime cannot tolerate the maintenance of even the simplest contacts between families and friends."

The following afternoon, infantry and armored units from all three Western occupation forces began patrolling right up to the border. The British pitched tents in the shadow of the rising wall, and a Patton tank with the name War Eagle painted on its turret hauled up to the Friedrichstrasse border crossing (soon to be dubbed "Checkpoint Charlie") and pointed its muzzle straight up the broad street.

Willy Brandt was delighted by this show of force, but also rueful: Why had it not been done ten days earlier? West Berliners in droves tendered their thanks to the French, British, and American units. But thanks weren't what the generals received from their chiefs back home.

In the White House, General Maxwell Taylor was alone in favoring action to assert the continuing authority of the Four-Power Agreements. From Paris, the word went out to General Lacomme that he was never again to deploy his troops without permission from the Quai d'Orsay. In London—or rather in Yorkshire, where he had remained during the unfolding crisis—Macmillan noted in his diary: "There is, actually, nothing illegal in the East Germans stopping the flow of refugees and putting themselves behind a still more rigid iron curtain. It certainly is not a very good advertisement for the benefits of Communism—but it is not (I believe) a breach of any of our agreements."

Macmillan erred. In fact, under the Four-Power Agreements, none of the occupying powers was authorized unilaterally to undertake a major change in the zone or sector under its administrative control. Yet the next day, accosted by newsmen on the golf course, Macmillan went further in expressing his indignation with those who refused to accept the border closing as a fait accompli. "I think it [the Berlin crisis] has been got up by the press," he said. And anyway, "Nobody is going to fight about it." This was not well received by West Berliners and their friends. And Macmillan sensed as much. The following day, he murmured discreetly to his diary, "I'm afraid I rather lost my temper with them [the press] and made some impromptu remarks which were given full front-page treatment in all the Sunday papers. It was undoubtedly a 'gaffe.'"

Khrushchev too was on vacation. But far from inactive. On August 29 he directed the Kremlin to announce that the scheduled release from active duty of Soviet reservists would be postponed. On August 30 the Kremlin announced that the Soviet Union would resume the atmospheric testing of nuclear weapons. The same day, discussing the Allies' refusal to negotiate on Berlin, Khrushchev told two visiting British MPs: "I have had enough. I am going to do something about it."

.   .   .

Day by day, the wall ascended. Ground-floor windows on Bernauerstrasse had been quickly bricked up; a few weeks later, masons, with a team of Vopos guarding them, went methodically down the street bricking up the higher windows until, finally, there was no place to jump from except the rooftops. The Communists then set about creating a no-man's-land, which became known as the "death strip." Where the border crossed an area of garden allotments, the Communists cut down fruit trees and ran bulldozers over the gardeners' cottages, achieving for the Vopos and Grepos a clear line of sight. One area that didn't need flattening was the site of Hitler's bunker. There, at the heart of the city, lay barren ground, with not so much as a tree or a shrub to adorn it.

It was to this stage of the Berlin crisis that General Clay returned on September 19. He and his wife, Marjorie, arrived at Tempelhof and were driven to the U.S. mission on Clayallee—named for him—through an honor guard of cheering Berliners.

That evening, the Clays were driven to Checkpoint Charlie. There they got out of the car, proceeded through the checkpoint to East Berlin, and started walking up Friedrichstrasse toward Unter den Linden, physically asserting the right of the Allies to be there. Even if the young Vopos at the checkpoint had no idea who their visitors were, the desired point had been made.

That evening walk set the tone for Clay's mission in Berlin. He had been sent to bolster the morale of the West Berliners, and they responded to him gleefully. They were delighted to have back in their midst the man who had saved West Berlin through the airlift and who symbolized the Allies' willingness to readmit post-Führer Germany into the civilized world.

A more dramatic confrontation was precipitated by Allan Lightner, who shared adamantly Clay's view that the Allies had to stand up to the Communists' violations. On the evening of Sunday, October 22, Lightner and his wife, Dorothy, set out for East Berlin to attend the theater. It was still routine for Americans to go into the eastern part of the city. Lightner knew, however, that for the past week the Communists had been ratcheting up their defiance of the Four-Power Agreements. They did this, first, by randomly demanding to see the identification papers of Allied officials at Checkpoint Charlie. A supplementary transgression was putting these spot checks in the hands of the Vopos. Soviet officers, as representatives of an occupying power, had general authority to regulate the border; not so, the East German police.

Lightner's car was stopped at the border by a Vopo. Lightner demanded to see a superintending Soviet officer. The Vopo argued. This went on for three-quarters of an hour, at which point Lightner said he was asserting his "Allied right" to enter any sector of Berlin. *"Get out of the way!"* Stepping on the gas, he scattered the Vopos. But ahead, his Volkswagen was slowed down by zigzagging barriers, and the Vopos were able to stop him again.

Someone on the scene telephoned the U.S. mission. Generals Watson and Clay were indignant at this fresh violation and dispatched two armored troop carriers and four medium-sized tanks (M-48s) to the checkpoint. An American MP left the little booth on the western side of the checkpoint and walked over to the besieged Volkswagen.

He suggested to Dorothy Lightner that she should get out of the car and await developments back at the checkpoint. She refused to leave her husband's side. The MP returned to his booth, made a telephone call, and then returned to the car. "General Clay *orders* Mrs. Lightner to get out." He then whispered, "We have a project in which we don't want Mrs. Lightner to be involved."

She left the car, and two infantry squads of four men each, armed with bayoneted rifles, walked through the checkpoint and took up positions on either side of the street. The tanks, on the American side of the border, pointed their muzzles up Friedrichstrasse. Flanked by the soldiers, Lightner eased the car into first gear and made his way past the barriers. He drove up the street a few blocks, proceeding at the same pace as his marching escort, then turned his car around and drove back to the checkpoint. On reaching the American side he turned around again. Once again the Vopos tried to stop him. He signaled to his armed escort, and together they repeated the sally. By the time they were back from this trip, a Soviet officer was on the scene. Lightner spotted him and set out for a third excursion, now followed by a car from the U.S. mission. This time the Vopos didn't interfere, and the U.S. expeditionary force went all the way to Unter den Linden and around by the Brandenburg Gate before heading back, triumphantly, to Checkpoint Charlie.

The next day, Monday, the East German government issued a new decree: All foreigners, excepting only American, French, or British officers in uniform, would henceforth be required to show identification papers to enter East Berlin. Acting on Clay's orders, two American military officers, dressed in civilian clothes and driving a car with U.S. plates, came up to Checkpoint Charlie. It was the Vopos who stopped them, but this time they had a Soviet officer on hand. As he and the American officer on duty argued, two more officials from the U.S. mission arrived. Anticipating a showdown, crowds were collecting on both sides of the border. General Clay ordered General Watson to dispatch ten M-48 tanks to the checkpoint. Over the next two days, the Americans sent convoys of civilian cars escorted by military jeeps through Checkpoint Charlie and up Friedrichstrasse, all of them making their way undisturbed.

This was a true stalemate. On Friday, October 27, Marshal Koniev, commander in chief of the Soviet forces in Germany, telephoned Khrushchev. What was he to do?

Match their ten tanks, said Khrushchev, *but don't fire first.*

At 10:00 P.M. Berlin time on Saturday the 28th, Clay and Watson were conferring in the U.S. mission's map room when Clay was called to the telephone: Washington was on the line. It was the president.

As Clay later recounted to the American historian Curtis Cate, Kennedy began by asking: "How are things up there?"

"We have ten tanks at Checkpoint Charlie," Clay replied. "The Russians have ten tanks there, too. So now we're equal." A note was handed to Clay. "Mr. President, I'll have to rectify that statement. The Russians have brought up twenty more tanks." There was something of levity in Clay's next words: "This is proof of the accuracy of their information. That is the number of tanks *we* have in Berlin. So we'll bring up our remaining twenty tanks as well."

"Tell me," the president said, "are you nervous?"

"Nervous?" said Clay. "No, we're not nervous here. If anybody's nervous, Mr. President, it will probably be people in Washington."

"Well," replied the president, "there may well be a lot of nervous people around here, but I'm not one of them."

The next day, Marshal Koniev (his nickname, as it happens, was "The Tank") phoned Moscow again. As Khrushchev later reported the conversation to a confidant, Koniev said he found the situation "grotesque." Khrushchev was now wary. "All right," he told his marshal. "Pull back your tanks. The Americans can't pull theirs back for reasons of prestige. So it's up to us to begin."

It was the first time in the Cold War that U.S. and Soviet tanks were face to face. And it would never happen again. Clay had hoped that the success of the confrontation would stiffen Washington's resolve, but Rusk & Sorensen & Schlesinger won the final round. Two weeks later, our ambassador to Moscow, Llewellyn Thompson, was preparing for talks with Foreign Minister Gromyko. He was instructed to convey to Gromyko that the West regarded the Berlin Wall as "a fact of international life."

The top British officials in Berlin favored sending Clay back to Cape Cod, and so did General Clarke, commander of the U.S. Army in Europe.

Clay's first adventure on this tour of duty, weeks before the tank episode, had been in Steinstücken. This community of two hundred souls was legally a part of West Berlin, but it was physically separated from the rest of the city by several miles of the Potsdam forest. Ever since August 13, it had been completely cut off, its residents forbidden to travel across the intervening strip of East German land.

Clay learned of Steinstücken's isolation his first day in Berlin and summoned a helicopter to go survey the scene. Within minutes of his arrival, what appeared to be all of Steinstücken had come out to greet him. He was led to meet the mayor, to whom he promised intervention. In a joyous lovefest, he told the Steinstückeners that he would be discussing their situation with Mayor Brandt, and that if they had any problems they should contact the U.S. occupation authorities directly. The next day, he sent another helicopter out with three American MPs, who remained in the village. Five days after that, he ordered that seven East Germans who had taken refuge in Steinstücken be transported to West Berlin proper.

By this time Ulbricht was apoplectic, and Clarke was on high alert. His concern, he later told Honoré Catudal, was the military defense of Free Europe, not the morale of West Berlin civilians. Given the preponderance of Communist military strength on the Continent, he reasoned that in a showdown over West Berlin, the city would have to be "sacrificed at once. There was no military way to save [it] without possibly a nuclear exchange between the U.S. and Russia." He saw it as part of his mandate to prevent anything that looked like provocation, and so, as he told Catudal, he was going to see to it that Clay kept his "cotton-picking fingers off my troops."

Notwithstanding Clarke's priorities and the lack of support from Washington, Clay stayed on for another seven months after the Checkpoint Charlie confrontation. Just before leaving, he was on the platform for West Berlin's May Day celebration. (In non-Communist Europe, May Day is their equivalent of Labor Day.) He was not scheduled to speak, but Brandt took the pulse of the crowd. One-third of the population of West Berlin was there, seven hundred thousand people. Brandt called Clay to the microphone. The crowd gave him an uproarious ovation. Clay told them, "I shall not now, or ever, say 'Good-bye.' For Berlin is too much a part of me to ever leave. I shall only say, as we say in America, 'So long, thank you, and God bless you.'"

The stream of refugees leaving East Berlin for West Berlin slowed drastically as the wall grew. Impromptu escapes of the kind made by Conrad Schumann or Georg and Carola Maurer became rare. But then the stream picked up again as a new vocation developed, that of "escape helper." The first organized method of escape, and the simplest, involved counterfeit identity cards. For a period after the seal-off, foreigners, and West Germans who were not citizens of West Berlin, were allowed to enter and leave East Berlin at will, merely upon showing their identity card. A network instantly sprang up at the Free University in West Berlin. It recruited students who had bona fide papers identifying them as citizens of West Germany, or France, or Italy, to visit East Berlin with an extra identity card tucked into a sock or their underwear. The extra card would be passed on to an East Berliner whose appearance roughly matched its photo.

Dozens escaped in this way before the Communists tightened the border controls. At that point, the refugees moved underground, to the municipal sewer system. Western accomplices—again, many of them university students—acquired maps, made contact with Easterners who wanted to escape, and led the way for them. This method succeeded for several months, but the Communists were hard at work, systematically installing heavy metal grilles across traversable passageways, and connecting the grilles to alarms. So . . . the escape helpers set out to dig fresh tunnels.

Some of the first tunnelers, however spirited in their enterprise, didn't know much about the requirements of tunnel-building. They were liberal-arts students who had little idea of how to provide ventilation, how to prevent flooding, or how to guard against noise or anything else that might attract attention. This didn't matter much at first, when the escape route was short, a matter of a few yards from the basement of a building just on the eastern side of the border to one just on the western side. But as the buildings that lay just on the eastern side were torn down, the tunnels needed to be longer, and amateur-hour construction was no longer good enough.

Tunneling entered a new phase in the matter of Peter Schmidt, a student trapped in East Berlin by the border closing. His friends at the Free University included a group of engineering students led by an Italian named Luigi Spina. Spina scouted assiduously to find terminuses for a tunnel, outgoing-incoming, that (a) were not too far apart, (b) would give ample cover, and (c) were in neighborhoods where a few extra people moving about would not arouse suspicion. He eventually made plans for a tube 15 feet below the surface, stretching 140 yards. It began within a deserted apartment building in the East and debouched into a factory in the West, on Bernauerstrasse. To avoid a disastrous collapse, Spina insisted on using proper wooden roof supports. By the time he and his accomplices had finished, 20 tons of wooden beams had been put into service. Air was piped in to the diggers, the dirt hauled out to the factory basement in electric carts.

A big problem was money. Students could not afford wood in that amount, or the equipment required. Some of the funds came in discreetly from anti-Communist groups and from corporate enterprises such as Axel Springer's media empire. The West Berlin government clandestinely funneled a few Marks to the tunnelers. But Spina ran out of cash when the tunnel was only one-quarter done. Enter NBC. Producer Reuven Frank had been looking for escape footage ever since the wall went up, and had told his Berlin correspondent, Piers Anderton, "Don't worry about getting any permission. Go ahead and do it. I'll pay the bill."

In the spring of 1962, Anderton told Frank about Spina's group and said they would need $50,000. Frank yelled, "They're trying to build a subway!" Eventually he bargained Spina down to $12,000, and began laying his plans to photograph the entire proceeding. It was a nerve-racking summer. First the weather was against the tunnelers: it rained so much in June as to threaten a collapse despite the wooden supports. Then a nearby water main broke. Fortunately, the break was in West Berlin, so it could be routinely reported to the authorities without risking the enterprise.

In September 1962 the tunnelers finally broke through. At noon on September 14, the fiancée of one of the diggers was dispatched to the East, using her legitimate West German papers, to round up the pilgrims who had been waiting so long. At 3:00 P.M., Frank's photographers went to the western end of the tunnel to wait for the first refugees to complete the crawl. It had been calculated that it would take 12 minutes to go the 140 yards, a little more than 10 yards a minute.

One by one the refugees appeared, muddy, bedraggled, and radiant. There were twenty-six of them, of all ages, from babes in arms to the elderly. The wife of one of the diggers emerged from the tunnel carrying their baby, who had been born in prison. In Frank's film, as edited for broadcasting, some of the faces were blacked out, to protect relatives left behind in the East. The *New York Times* covered the story. "In their wet and mud-spattered clothing and in their expressions of relief," wrote the *Times*'s reviewer, Jack Gould, "there was a telling indictment of life under Communism. That they would take such risks and hardship to escape spoke for itself." The tunnel was used again the following Sunday for thirty-one more escapees, but almost immediately afterward it was closed down, not by the Vopos but by a final flood.

When the Spina crew was only halfway along in its tunneling, a very different kind of escape attempt took place. It seared into memory as live testimony to the West's incapacity to deal with the wall. On August 17, 1962, two eighteen-year-old construction workers trusted to the element of surprise. They set out in broad daylight, at a little after 2:00 P.M., to the wall, with the clear design of climbing over it. One of them made it; the guards shot the second one, just as he was reaching the top of the wall. He fell back on the eastern side.

The Vopos did nothing: they did not fire a second bullet, ending the young man's pain, nor did they cart him away. He was left lying in the sun, bleeding to death and screaming for help within earshot of a gathering crowd on the western side of the wall, and within sight of Checkpoint Charlie. According to German witnesses, some American soldiers set about to give help, but their officers stopped them. They would not let them risk an "incident." General Watson, who had collaborated with Clay in confronting the East German tanks, would not send men across the border now without authorization. He was at least willing to break the chain of command, circumventing two echelons of generals to call the White House directly. Watson was still, so to speak, on the phone waiting for permission to help the bleeding German when, at 3:05 P.M., the Vopos walked over and dragged the body away. Peter Fechter, who became a legend, was dead.

By late 1962, another front in the Cold War was moving, menacingly, in. On October 19, the White House received, as McGeorge Bundy put it, "hard photographic evidence" that the Russians had "offensive missiles in Cuba."

This shouldn't have come as a surprise. Cuban exile

leaders had been warning of the Soviet initiative for weeks; so had Republican Senator Kenneth Keating of New York and Richard Nixon, campaigning for governor of California. Even if the administration didn't believe *them,* the West had a spy, critically situated: Colonel Oleg Penkovsky, of Soviet military intelligence. In early July, Penkovsky presented his British contact, Greville Wynne, with current operations manuals giving comprehensive information on the SS-4 and SS-5 IRBMs (intermediate-range ballistic missiles) that Khrushchev would be sending the Cubans in just a few weeks' time. Through it all, until Bundy's "hard photographic evidence" was received, the administration kept insisting that the objects that Soviet ships were transporting to the Caribbean were merely "defensive anti-aircraft weapons."

Forced to confront reality, the president spent three days with his closest advisers, the "Excom" (Executive Committee of the National Security Council), hammering out what he would (a) do, and (b) say to the American people. When he went on television on Monday, October 22, he spoke of an "urgent transformation of Cuba into an important strategic base by the presence of these large long-range and clearly offensive weapons." They constituted, the president said, "an explicit threat to the peace and security of all the Americas." He outlined a plan for a "quarantine on all offensive military equipment under shipment to Cuba" and called upon Chairman Khrushchev "to abandon this course of world domination and to join in an historic effort to end the perilous arms race and to transform the history of man." He concluded by advising his "fellow citizens" that "the cost of freedom is always high, but Americans have always paid it." For the first time since the Cold War began, many level-headed Americans went about their lives less than entirely sure that nuclear war didn't lie directly ahead.

On October 24, the first Soviet ships approached the quarantine line. An aide interrupted the Excom meeting to hand CIA director John McCone, Allen Dulles's successor, a note saying that the Soviet ships seemed to be stopping. Seven minutes later, the report was confirmed: the ships were turning back. Dean Rusk murmured to McGeorge Bundy: "We're eyeball to eyeball and I think the other fellow just blinked."

In fact, it was a classic Soviet maneuver, two steps forward, one step back. The IRBMs did get carted back to the Soviet Union. But other matériel—including tanks, MiG fighters, radar batteries, and a "fishing fleet" in Havana Harbor—remained. President Kennedy in effect abandoned the interpretation of the Monroe Doctrine that forbade interference by a European power in the Western Hemisphere. This, by guaranteeing, in return for the removal of the IRBMs, that Cuba would not be invaded.

Coloring all the calculations of the president and his men was—Berlin. During those days of continuous Excom deliberations, JFK's second-greatest fear, after full-scale nuclear war, was that any action he might take would lead Khrushchev to retaliate against West Berlin.

President Kennedy had all along assumed a link between the Communist outpost in the Caribbean and the Western outpost behind the Iron Curtain. In April 1961, Richard Nixon had paid a visit to the White House and counseled

his successful rival for the presidency to respond to the failure of the Bay of Pigs operation with a full-scale invasion
of Cuba. "I would find proper legal cover and I would go
in," the former vice president advised. Kennedy demurred:
"There is a good chance that if we move on Cuba,
Khrushchev will move on Berlin." Now, against the contingency that, as part of the action during the Missile Crisis, the Soviets again cut off Berlin, he had the Excom plan
another Berlin airlift. The wording of his October 22
address to the nation took account of the Berlin connection. Sorensen urged him to refer to the American
response as a "quarantine." Avoid the word "blockade":
that's what *they* do. After outlining the quarantine,
Kennedy reinforced the distinction he wanted to draw:
"We are not at this time, however, denying the necessities
of life, as the Soviets attempted to do in their Berlin blockade of 1948." The words were pointed, and the West
waited. But, it seemed, the Soviets' aggressive energies
were spent, for the time being.

Castro's Cuba remained, in President Kennedy's words,
a "dagger pointed at the heart of America," and Berlin
remained the bone in Nikita Khrushchev's throat.

3

In the Shadow of the Wall

Another eight months went by before President Kennedy visited the city that had taken up so much of his attention. In June 1963 he set off on a ten-day visit to Europe, a trip adroitly described by James Burnham as "a grand campaign tour" in his "contest with President de Gaulle" over the future of NATO. His speeches in West Germany were directly aimed at countering de Gaulle's repeated assertions that the United States—quite understandably, the general often added—would never risk its own cities to defend Western Europe's, and, therefore, Western Europe needed its own deterrent nuclear force.

In acknowledging Chancellor Adenauer's welcome at Wahn Airport, halfway between Cologne and Bonn, President Kennedy gave a direct affirmation of U.S. loyalty to Europe and did so in aphoristic language. "Your safety is our safety, your liberty is our liberty, and any attack on your soil is an attack on our soil. . . . [O]ur fortunes are one." In a major address in Frankfurt he amplified on the point. "The United States," he averred, "will risk its cities to defend yours because we need your freedom to protect ours. Hundreds of thousands of our soldiers serve with yours on this continent, as tangible evidence of this pledge. Those who would doubt our pledge or deny this indivisibility—those who would separate Europe from America or split one ally from another—would only give aid and comfort to . . . our adversaries."

The next day, June 26, accompanied by Chancellor Adenauer and General Clay, Kennedy flew from Wiesbaden to West Berlin. They were met by Willy Brandt at Tegel Airport and driven through a city more than half of whose inhabitants lined the streets hoping to have a glimpse of the young president. There were no protesters out, asking why the United States had abandoned half of Berlin. The august party made several stops. At the Brandenburg Gate a viewing platform had been designed high enough to permit the president to look over the wall into East Berlin.

Clay worried about a possible attempt on the president's life, but Kennedy brushed aside the general's concerns and walked up the steps to the platform. Having got there, he wasn't able to see much of the East—Ulbricht's men had blocked the arches of the gate with great lengths of blood-red cloth. Still, Kennedy had made his formal appearance. The party then drove to City Hall, where 150,000 cheering Berliners had gathered in Rudolf Wilde Platz. Here, after relentless coaching by McGeorge Bundy ("I guess I ought to leave the foreign languages to Jackie," he had said ruefully), JFK uttered some of the most resonant words of his presidency: "Two thousand years ago the proudest boast was 'Civis Romanus sum.' Today in the world of freedom the proudest boast is 'Ich bin ein Berliner.'" The cheers almost stopped him. But he went on: "There are many people in the world who really don't understand—or say they don't—what is the great issue between the free world and the Communist world. Let them come to Berlin."

The president was in high anaphoric gear. "There are some who say that Communism is the wave of the future. Let them come to Berlin. And there are some who say in Europe and elsewhere, 'We can work with the Communists.' Let them come to Berlin. And there are even a few who say that it's true that Communism is an evil system but it permits us to make economic progress. Let them come to Berlin.

"Freedom has many difficulties, and democracy is not perfect. But we have never had to put a wall up to keep our people in, to prevent them from leaving us. All free men, wherever they may live, are citizens of Berlin. And therefore, as a free man, I take pride in the words 'Ich bin ein Berliner.'"

Poor Walter Ulbricht. The secretary-general would turn seventy on June 30, and JFK's visit seemed almost calculated to spoil his birthday. But Nikita Khrushchev exerted himself to counter the unseemly demonstrations on the other side of the wall. He arrived in East Berlin on the 28th, two days earlier than scheduled, and was driven into the city through a crowd of two hundred thousand. Khrushchev was in fine form. In an off-the-cuff talk to a group of factory workers, he noted that Kennedy had been offended by the wall. "But me," said the chairman, "I like it. It pleases me tremendously. The working class of

Germany has erected a wall so that no wolf can break into the German Democratic Republic again. Is that bad?" At the birthday reception itself, Khrushchev declared that "Germany will not be reunited in our time—unless it becomes Socialist." Turning to the guest of honor, he added: "May you live two hundred years, and then we could discuss again how things are going."

Ulbricht had done much to earn the Soviet ruler's backing. He had been wholehearted in his support of the Kremlin in the developing rift with Red China. Even Mrs. Ulbricht, who preferred to stay in the background, had spoken out, replying spiritedly to the leader of the Chinese delegation to the World Women's Congress in Moscow. But then, world affairs were a welcome respite from the day-to-day problems of ruling a nation so many of whose people made it all too clear on which side of the wall they would prefer to be.

The Ulbricht regime worked steadily on strengthening the wall—making it higher, topping every bit of it with barbed wire, beefing up the security measures in the death strip. Such escapes as succeeded in the mid-1960s were nearly all organized enterprises, usually done with an experienced "escape helper" in charge. The king of the escape helpers, responsible for rescuing several hundred people, was a man known as "Tunnel Fuchs."

Wolfgang Fuchs was not yet twenty when, in August 1961, he contrived to bring out from the East his young wife, an East German citizen who happened to be visiting her family on the day the border was sealed. That first escape was relatively simple, back before the concrete replaced the original barbed wire, but escape engineering became a misson for Fuchs. He spent the next thirteen years of his life as a full-time escape helper. He was one of the first to organize the forging of identity cards, and then to help map the sewer system. As that egress was, in turn, systematically closed off, he started digging escape tunnels.

The digging part was always tense, owing to the possibility of accident (as with the repeated flooding of Luigi Spina's tunnel) and of enemy intervention. The Stasi had some success at infiltrating the ranks of the diggers. Once, just as Fuchs's crew was about to break through on the eastern side, the Stasi, having discovered the tunnel, dropped a bomb into the shaft. If the diggers had happened to be closer than they were to the eastern end, they would have been killed by the explosion in a confined space.

But digging was also exhilarating. At the beginning, when fresh ground was apprehensively broken, there was a thrill, which culminated when, however many days or weeks or months later, the diggers reached the eastern destination. Fuchs later told the British historian Anthony Kemp, "I believe that I have seldom been so happy in my life, however corny that may sound, [as] when I was down there. I always sang. . . . When one is underground for ten days under the Wall and drills and digs, and another cubic metre of earth has been cleared, one gets another step forward. That is a dreamlike feeling."

The danger didn't end when a tunnel was completed. At that point, exit schedules were drawn up. Couriers with foreign or West German (but never West Berlin) papers would cross over into the East and meet their refugee-clients, who had previously petitioned for sponsorship through agents trusted by Fuchs. The courier would give the client a meeting place, date, time, and password. Some clients intended to flee alone, others as couples. Still others intended to bring with them young children or aged parents.

On the designated evening, couriers would meet the clients, one person or family at a time. After the client had given the password, the courier would disclose the address of the building that housed the eastern end of the tunnel.

Fuchs would be watching the client with binoculars from a roof on the western side. If he spotted no Vopo or Stasi tail, he would radio to his crew on the eastern side to open the outside door. After an interval of several minutes, the procedure would be repeated on behalf of another client. On no account would a suspicious aggregation of people be permitted at the entrance to the tunnel.

After the client had successfully made the crawl and had climbed up the ladder to freedom, his identity would be verified once more. Papers were not always needed, or expected. Often the diggers were working to free a wife, a brother, a close friend.

The clients would then have to be cleaned up before being released onto the street. In that city of lakes, rivers, and canals, the water table was never low enough to free the tunnels of mud. Fuchs described his own reaction to the end of a successful tunneling operation: "I must say that the most beautiful feeling was for me to see when the people came crawling out of the tunnel, on their knees from East Berlin like mice. I can never forget. The marks of their kneeprints in the tunnel floor looked like the ripples on a beach left behind by the receding tide. It does not matter what may become of me, I will never forget that. That is beautiful and that is happiness."

From happiness to disaster. On the nights of October 3 and 4, 1964, fifty-seven people emerged from one of Fuchs's tunnels. Just after midnight on the second night, two men arrived at the eastern building not knowing the password. They seemed frightened, though, and the students guarding the entrance believed they were genuine refugees. Having been acknowledged, the men said they had to go back to reassure a friend. He had got cold feet, it was explained, but would certainly now join them.

When they returned with the third man, he proved to be a uniformed soldier. The students pulled out their guns and started firing. The East Germans returned their fire. The students escaped, but the soldier died. Whether from a student bullet or from a misdirected shot by his collaborators was not known, at least not to the West Berlin authorities. In any case, although those authorities refused extradition demands, they did crack down on tunneling. Fuchs had to devise new escape methods.

The most picturesque of these was the hinged ladder. Fuchs had read about the jailbreak of a British train robber. The robber's confederates had driven to the prison in a furniture truck and contrived to hang a ladder over a side wall; the prisoner climbed the ladder, dropped through a hole in the truck's roof, and was off. For the escape of Jürgen Kummer, Fuchs & Company selected a cemetery that abutted on the Berlin Wall. Patient surveillance disclosed that the cemetery contained a blind spot, not visible from any of the watchtowers. Kummer traveled several times over the course of a few weeks to visit a grave near the planned escape site, so that his appearance there was now accepted as a regular rite. On the designated day, there was the ladder, and over he went.

The plan worked perfectly—once. After Kummer's escape, the Communists dug up all the graves near the wall and created, morbidly, a death strip within the cemetery. No more cemetery life.

Fuchs then turned to other forms of motorized transport. Many other escape helpers had successfully used vehicles in their efforts. Some of the cars used were improbably small, able to conceal only a quite diminutive refugee. But enough of those attempts had succeeded to bring stern surveillance from the East Germans. The Grepos started searching minutely every nonofficial car crossing the border. They took to tapping fenders to make sure they were hollow, using heat detectors to find hidden compartments, passing a mirror underneath the car, and ripping up seats.

So? Since this was how civilian cars were treated, Fuchs arranged to use an official car. He found a Syrian diplomat who desperately wanted his own car but was short on funds. Fuchs gave him a secondhand Mercedes. In return, the Syrian ferried refugees across the border in his trunk. Eventually he was betrayed and expelled from East Berlin as persona non grata.

Fuchs's last effort was the "Supercar." Its secret has not been revealed, but according to Kemp, it was "a large American vehicle that could be subjected to the most rigorous search including virtual demolition at a frontier post." Its hiding place "was most uncomfortable and cramped for the person within." The car made a number of successful runs before it and its owner both retired. Fatigue and material necessity. The Superman Escape Angel put the car away in an undisclosed location in West Germany and took up the trade of pharmacist to make a living for his family, looking, for once, to his own concerns.

By the time of Fuchs's last tunnel, in October 1964, the dramatis personae at the highest political level had nearly all changed. Macmillan's government had been severely wounded by the Profumo scandal in the spring of 1963, in which the Right Honorable Member lied to Commons about the sex story in which he was involved. It is relevant that his girlfriend, Christine Keeler, was also carrying on an affair with the Soviet naval attaché. Soviet naval attachés were always inquisitive about their host country.

Then Macmillan was diagnosed with prostate cancer, giving him a way to resign gracefully. He would return to the family book-publishing business and to the writing of long, chatty, often waspishly witty memoirs. He withdrew as prime minister in favor of Alec Douglas-Home—"Sir Alec," he had been reduced to, forswearing his seat in the House of Lords in order to serve. But it was only for a short time. Twelve months after heading up the ruling Tory Party, Douglas-Home led it to defeat at the polls, on October 15, 1964.

Adenauer's government also had been wounded, though less severely, by political scandal—in this case, allegations that the chancellor's closest aide, Hans Globke, had been a Nazi engaged in war crimes. (Globke maintained that he had stayed on at his post in Hitler's Interior Ministry only in order to soften Nazi measures against the Jews.) And then as de Gaulle drew further and further away from the United States, detaching France from the NATO military command and even seeking a rapprochement with Moscow, some of Adenauer's Christian Democratic colleagues became nervous about Der Alte's closeness to le grand Charles. Adenauer resisted for a period but finally gave way, resigning on October 15, 1963.

The week before, he paid a farewell visit to Berlin. He reiterated his warnings against the West's pending deal to sell wheat to Russia ("Only the stupidest calves choose their own butcher"), but then said that if the Allies insisted on going through with the sale, they should at least get something besides money for their goods. Something dear to the heart of West Germans: "The Russians must be told that in return for the food they need, the wall must go."

Adenauer was succeeded by the man who had served him as minister of economics throughout his fourteen years as chancellor, and who was given much of the credit for "the German Miracle," the recovery from postwar wasteland to one of the most productive industrial states in the world. Ludwig Erhard was a thoroughly German figure, self-possessed, loyal, hardworking. He was later asked why he had so compliantly absorbed public rebuffs from the acid-tongued Adenauer. He answered that "For human and political reasons I could not move against the eighty-seven-year-old man." Adenauer would spend another four years in his Rhöndorf garden, dying at age ninety-one.

In October 1964, while Nikita Khrushchev was vacationing at his Black Sea retreat, his colleagues moved against him as, eleven years earlier, he had moved against Lavrenty Beria. There was for Khrushchev the consolation that his successors did not shoot him, as he had had Beria shot. He was moved into an apartment in one of those massive squalid gray buildings in Moscow—I once saw his laundry hanging from his balcony. He died in 1971 at age seventy-seven, apparently of natural causes.

It was of course not so with the other great critical figure of the time. John F. Kennedy, the glamorous young president of the United States, the honorary Berliner, did not die of natural causes, his bloody death being one of the most pondered and debated events of a bloody century. At the reception following his funeral, Jacqueline Kennedy thanked Willy Brandt for renaming Rudolf Wilde Platz. The scene of her husband's famous speech would now be John F. Kennedy Platz. Escorting Brandt out to his car after the reception, Bobby told the mayor, "He loved Berlin."

One reason why the Western authorities stopped supporting Tunnel Fuchs was that, after two years of non-communication, the Ulbricht regime had entered into negotiations with West Germany. The principal fruit of the first East–West talks was the Passierschein (visiting permit) agreement of December 1963. It allowed West Berliners to acquire temporary passes to visit relatives in the East for Christmas. Over the next few years these golden passes would be made available, off and on—for a price. Even so, Western visitors were only cautiously received. They were allowed to stay in East Berlin for just a single day, and they had to apply for each visit at least two days in advance.

Non-Germans also were allowed to visit, for a fee, although probationally. A guidebook of the time warned that the information it provided about visiting East Berlin "is given without any guarantee of its continuing validity."

Far more lucrative for Ulbricht's regime was a scheme thought up by East Berlin lawyer Wolfgang Vogel: Freikauf (ransom). In return for cash money, or for credits for badly needed goods—butter, coffee, medicines, machine tools— East Germany would release to the West individual political prisoners designated by Bonn.

It was Willy Brandt who had set in motion the search for a way to free political prisoners. Every day, as mayor, he had to deal with the same heartache, constituents whose families had been divided by the wall. As early as the spring of 1962, Dietrich Spangenberg, an assistant of Brandt's, made contact with a West Berlin attorney, Jürgen Stange, who had frequently worked with Vogel on cross-border matters. Stange now brought Spangenberg to meet Vogel. When Spangenberg outlined the mayor's agenda, Vogel quickly saw the solution. "Children," he said avuncularly, "you know that our economy is not in the best of shape. Maybe you could pay to regulate this traffic."

Spangenberg's next assignment was to sound out Bonn. He went first to Franz Thedieck, an official at the Ministry for All-German Affairs. Thedieck was outraged. "How can you equate people with money?" he thundered.

So Spangenberg and Stange made an end run around the bureaucracy. Stange obtained an introduction to press lord Axel Springer. Springer liked the Freikauf idea and put it to Thedieck's boss, Rainer Barzel. Barzel in turn put it to Der Alte, who swiftly approved it. It took time to work out the details, but in August 1964 the first dozen ransomed prisoners were taken by bus from East Germany to a refugee center at Giessen, near Frankfurt.

The Adenauer government and successor governments, whether led by Christian Democrats or Social Democrats, approved of the scheme, but everyone agreed that it must be shrouded in secrecy. In West Germany's federal budget, Freikauf was listed as "support of special aid measures of an all-German character." The Lutheran Church agreed to launder the money.

When word nonetheless leaked out, Joachim Bölke, editor of the independent West Berlin daily *Der Tagesspiegel,* wrote that it was "a dreadful slave trade," in which the West German government was "descending to the level of the opposition." Springer instructed the editor of his *Berliner Morgenpost* to counterattack. "Our readers will understand," said the *Morgenpost* editorial, "when we—in the interest of political prisoners who are still awaiting release and regardless of the behavior of other media— maintain silence in this matter. . . . There is news that in fact kills, while affecting only to inform."

On the other side of the wall, Josef Streit, a high-level functionary in the East German Department of Justice, explained his government's justification for accepting ransom: This was, you see, compensation for the money the Democratic Republic had spent on educating people whose services would now be lost to it.

And so, despite the uneasiness on both sides, Freikauf remained a feature of German life through Cold War, détente, and Ostpolitik, right up to the end of the German division. In twenty-six years it effected the release of twenty-five thousand political prisoners, for whom the West paid a total of 5 billion Marks (about $2 billion).

Vogel had initially come to the West's attention through a different sort of ransoming: the first of the spy exchanges consummated so dramatically on the Glienecke Bridge. This bridge, which the Eastern authorities, with their wonderful verbal ingenuity, renamed the Bridge of Socialist Unity, does not run between what was then East and West Berlin. It crosses the Havel River between the southwestern edge of West Berlin and East Germany proper.

The man known as Colonel Rudolf Abel had been a spy for the Soviet Union in the United States for eight years, sending out, from his photographic studio in Brooklyn, New York, information on bits of microfilm concealed in issues of *Better Homes and Gardens*. He had finally been caught (through betrayal by a confederate), tried, and convicted, and was serving a thirty-year sentence in a federal prison in Texas. The Soviets proposed a one-for-one trade: Abel for Francis Gary Powers, the U-2 pilot shot down over Soviet territory in 1960.

The Soviets looked to the GDR to stage-manage the trade, and the GDR turned to Vogel. He contacted Abel's court-appointed defense lawyer, a successful, politically ambitious Brooklynite named James B. Donovan. Donovan now got in touch with the White House and was given the go-ahead—unofficially. As his contact explained, Washington confronted a diplomatically forbidden situation: dealing with a government it did not recognize. The contact did at least say that if anything "went wrong," Washington would take the matter very seriously "on the highest level."

On February 2, 1962, Donovan flew to West Berlin. The next day he took the S-Bahn to the Friedrichstrasse Station, and made his way to the Soviet embassy. After two days of frustrating conversations with embassy official Ivan Shishkin, he went to meet Vogel. It took the two lawyers several days to work out the details, because of jockeying between East Berlin and Moscow over how any exchange was actually to be effected. But they finally cut through the difficulties.

On the morning of Saturday, February 10, Shishkin and two embassy colleagues walked to the middle of the Glienicke Bridge, where they met Donovan and Allan Lightner. After a few formalities, Donovan and Shishkin waved to their respective sides' guards, who came forward escorting prisoner Francis Gary Powers, whose view of the Communist world until he was shot down had been from 80,000 feet in his U-2, and prisoner Rudolf Abel. Amid the imposing girders of the historic bridge, the exchange was completed.

Two years later, a Glienecke exchange was arranged involving Colonel Penkovsky's old British contact, Greville Wynne. Penkovsky and Wynne had both been arrested by the KGB soon after Penkovsky passed along the information about Soviet missiles heading for Cuba. Penkovsky was tried as a traitor and forthwith executed; Wynne was tried as a spy and sentenced to eight years in prison. He was kept under conditions harsh even by Soviet standards, apparently with a view to persuading the British to ransom him. They did this in 1964, agreeing to give up the Soviet spymaster known in the West as Gordon Lonsdale.

One of the last exchanges, in February 1986, was among the most dramatic. In this case it was not two high-ranking spies. It was half a dozen assorted spies and one man who had been jailed as a spy but was not: the celebrated Jewish refusenik Anatoly Shcharansky. The logistics were easier than they had been in the Abel-Powers exchange, in that we now had diplomatic relations with East Germany, and Vogel was able to work directly with our ambassador to East Berlin, Francis Meehan. However, arrangements were complicated precisely by the fact that Shcharansky was not a spy and our side did not want him perceived as one. Accordingly, Vogel and Meehan kept Shcharansky segregated until the actual spies had been exchanged. Then they walked to the middle of the bridge with their special charge. The television cameras rolling, they handed the diminutive computer scientist over to our ambassador to Bonn, Richard Burt, and West German official Ludwig Rehlinger, who twenty-two years earlier had had a hand in working out the Freikauf arrangements.

West Berlin, in the shadow of the wall, seemed insular, isolated. "We're cozy here by our wall," one citizen commented. It might have been expected that the great wave of student riots, which had begun in the United States in the 1960s and traveled seemingly everywhere, would bypass the city. After all, young West Berliners were in no danger of being called up and sent to Vietnam. In fact, they weren't in danger of being called up at all. Because of

West Berlin's peculiar legal status, West Berliners were not subject to military service. Many young people migrated to the city for just that reason, to avoid military service in West Germany.

Many of them were left-oriented, and they were attracted to every cause that sprang up on the world scene—Algeria, apartheid, Vietnam. The riot that ended the long period of postwall solidarity was not set off by anything that affected Germans, let alone Berliners, directly. What did it was a visit by, of all people, the shah of Iran. There was, of course, the attitudinal unpopularity of the shah, always something of a cause among the left. But now his wife, Empress Farah, had published an article in the German magazine *Neue Revue*. In what must have seemed to her and the editors an innocuous passage, she had written, "Summers are very hot in Iran, and like most Persians I and my family travel to the Persian Riviera on the Caspian Sea."

One West Berlin journalist, a young woman named Ulrike Meinhof, did not find the passage innocuous. "'Like most Persians'—isn't that somewhat exaggerated?" Meinhof hit down in a widely circulated pamphlet. "Most Persians are peasants with an annual income of less than $100." As for the children of poor families, who, Meinhof went on, "knot carpets in their fourteen-hour day—do they too, most of them, travel to the Persian Riviera on the Caspian Sea in the summer?"

When the shah and his empress arrived in West Berlin on June 2, 1967, the streets were lined with supporters and detractors. Despite a heavy police presence, pockets of fighting broke out. As the fighting spread, police, using truncheons and turning firehoses on the demonstrators, started making arrests. Then came the flare point. A plain-clothes policeman fired a shot that killed a twenty-six-year-old graduate student named Benno Ohnesorg. West Berlin had its Kent State.

Ohnesorg's death quickly spawned a terrorist group called the June 2 Movement, and another that styled itself the Red Army Faction, after the Japanese terrorist group.

On the morning of May 14, 1970, two guards escorted an inmate from his prison in West Berlin to the German Central Institute for Social Issues. The inmate was Andreas Baader, the twenty-seven-year-old leader of the Red Army Faction. Baader was serving a four-year sentence for "arson endangering human life." He had received permission to work on a book about "organizing young people on the fringes of society." He also had received permission to employ a literary assistant, and he chose Ulrike Meinhof. As Baader and Meinhof conferred over books and notes that morning, three confederates arrived at the institute and shot the elderly librarian; they then ushered their leader and his new "assistant" out to a waiting Alfa Romeo. On June 2, the Red Army Faction issued a communiqué using fundamentalist revolutionary language of the kind, across the Atlantic, associated with Eldridge Cleaver. "Did the pigs really believe that we would let Comrade Baader sit in jail for two or three years? Did any pig really believe we would talk about the development of class struggle, the reorganization of the proletariat, without arming ourselves at the same time? . . . Whoever does not defend himself will die. Start the armed resistance! Build up the Red Army!"

The Red Army Faction became known as the Baader–Meinhof Gang, although Meinhof was not actually the second in command. That office was held by Baader's girlfriend, Gudrun Ensslin, who had reacted to the shooting of Benno Ohnesorg by denouncing the "fascist state" and "the generation of Auschwitz." But whether as the Red Army Faction or the Baader–Meinhof Gang, the Berlin-born group terrorized West Germany for the next seven years, robbing banks to support the revolution and killing people who got in the way. Baader and Ensslin were captured in 1972, whereupon gang members on the loose started kidnapping and killing with the express purpose of forcing the government to release their leaders. Their most prominent victim was the president of West Berlin's highest court, Günter von Drenkmann, shot dead in 1974. When, in 1977, a West German anti-terrorist unit spectacularly foiled an airplane hijacking by Palestinians sympathetic to Baader–Meinhof, the imprisoned Baader and Ensslin committed suicide, and the movement quickly disintegrated. (Meinhof had committed suicide the previous year.) Surviving members of this and other radical West German groups went, mostly, into Green politics, further complicating the Cold War scene.

In Paris, the worldwide student revolt accomplished what army officers outraged by the abandonment of Algeria could not: it toppled Charles de Gaulle.

The trouble began on May 2, 1968, when a handful of students led by Daniel Cohn-Bendit—dubbed Danny the Red, both for his politics and for the color of his hair—

occupied a lecture hall at the Nanterre campus of the University of Paris to protest "imperialism." The next day, a thousand students attempted to occupy the Sorbonne campus in sympathy. When the police started to remove them, a riot ensued.

The wave of demonstrations and riots continued through the next week. On May 13, both the Communist-led and the Catholic-led labor unions called a twenty-four-hour general strike to express solidarity with the students. Workers across the country seized factories and raised red flags. At the height of the strike, ten million workers and civil servants were on the picket line—one-third of France's workforce.

On May 24 de Gaulle judged the time ripe for a dramatic appeal and called for a referendum, a national vote of confidence. "Over a period of thirty years," he told the nation in a televised speech, "events have imposed upon me, on several grave occasions, the duty of leading our country to assume its own destiny so as to prevent some from taking that responsibility, despite its will. I am ready to do so, this time again. But, this time again, this time above all, I need—yes, I need—the French people to tell me that this is their wish."

In past crises, similar speeches by de Gaulle had produced almost magical results. Not so this time. The students headed back to the streets, and the workers stayed out on strike. On May 29, de Gaulle secretly flew to Baden-Baden to meet with General Jacques Massu, who had led the French in the Battle of Algiers in 1957 and who was now commander in chief of the French forces stationed in West Germany. De Gaulle wanted to discuss contingency plans in case he finally deemed a military solution necessary.

On the evening of May 30 de Gaulle again took to the airwaves—radio only, this time, because the strikes had immobilized the television system. Speaking from the Elysée Palace, he told the French people that the proposed referendum would have to be postponed until "civic action" had been restored. He finished his short speech (it took less than five minutes) with the words, "The Republic shall not abdicate."

This time the effect was electric. Ordinary Frenchmen took to the streets, not to riot but to declare their loyalty to the general. More than a million people filled the Champs-Elysées—double the largest crowd the Communists had assembled during the month's unrest. Long before they dispersed to their homes that night, it was clear that de Gaulle would remain in power. But only for a few months. The following April, he lost the referendum and ceased "to exercise my functions as president of the Republic."

Now Ulbricht and Brandt were the only leading actors of 1961 still in positions of power.

Prague was one major city that *was* spared student rebellions. There, it was fully grown adults who were rebelling, and not against the government, but from within it. In January 1968, Alexander Dubcek was elected first secretary of the Communist Party, replacing the old Stalinist Antonin Novotny, who had held the post since 1953.

Dubcek was a lifelong Communist. He insisted that the reforms he proposed were intended not to weaken but to strengthen the Communist movement. "Our friends [in the Soviet Politburo] will understand—even if not at once—that the Czechoslovakian regeneration process does not threaten the interests" of the Soviet Bloc, he said in a speech in July 1968. "On the contrary, it is the only possible way to make our republic a really solid part of the Socialist establishment."

Whatever Dubcek's subjective intentions, his program, as the Soviet Politburo understood all too well, could only lead to a slackening of the central authority on which a Communist state depends. He proposed loosening press censorship; giving the courts, the trade unions, and various economic enterprises increased autonomy; and permitting a measure of political freedom for four non-Communist parties. To keep a nation's writers in line requires total control by the state, writers being, generically, expressive creatures who do not conform unless required to do so. And, sure enough, even the official newspaper of the Czechoslovakian Communist Party, *Rude Pravo,* described Warsaw Pact criticism of the Czechoslovakian liberalization as "one of the old bad habits" of Communist regimes.

The fraternal Warsaw Pact countries gave Dubcek every possible chance. At an emergency summit meeting in Dresden on March 23, 1968, his fellow CP first secretaries gently explained that if he continued improving relations with *West* Germany, it would have a negative effect on relations with *East* Germany, as also with Poland. On July 29, nearly the entire Soviet Politburo, led by Leonid Brezhnev and Aleksei Kosygin, traveled to Cierna, a town in Slovakia, for three and a half days of meetings with the Czechoslovakian Presidium, led by Dubcek. Those meetings paved the way for a meeting on August 3 in Bratislava that was widened to include top Party and government officials from East Germany, Poland, Hungary, and Bulgaria. The communiqué that came out of the Bratislava meeting made some concessions to Dubcek. Acknowledged was the need to take "into consideration the national specific features and conditions" of each of the Eastern Bloc countries. However, the communiqué also made clear that "it is possible to advance along the road of Socialism and Communism only by being strictly and consistently guided by the general laws of construction of Socialist society and, primarily, by consolidating the leading role of the working class and its vanguard—the Communist parties."

Dubcek had complained to some townsfolk in Cierna, "We are dealing with people we call brothers, but we cannot get through to them." On the night of August 20–21, the Soviets got through to Dubcek—with 200,000 troops. They invaded their sister country, coming in from East Germany, Poland, Hungary, and Ukraine, with military forces predominantly Soviet, but including token forces from other Warsaw Pact countries. By the following week, the size of the invading force had swelled to 650,000.

Czechoslovakian students, who hadn't rebelled before, now had ripe reason to do so. They squatted down in front of tanks, painted swastikas on military vehicles, and publicly posted license-plate numbers of Soviet secret police. Some twenty thousand Czechs of all ages gathered in Prague's Wenceslaus Square and shouted out their cry, "Russian murderers go home!" at soldiers armed with bayoneted rifles. Three times, resisters derailed trains bringing to Prague special equipment designed to locate clandestine radio transmitters. There was even some sniper activity. But with no prospect of help from outside, there was no substantial armed resistance.

The Soviets too were warier than they had been in invading Hungary in 1956. They responded to individual incidents with specific punishments, not wholesale retaliation. They did not even oust Dubcek immediately, permitting him to stay on as first secretary until April 1969 and to hold his government posts until October of that year.

But his effort "to create a socialism that has not lost its human character" had been definitively halted. The Prague Spring was ended, and the Brezhnev Doctrine was born: *Once a Communist nation, always a Communist nation.* East Germany 1953, Hungary 1956, Czechoslovakia 1968. There would be local disturbances here and there, but it would be another decade before the Captive Nations, as we called them, seriously stirred again. In West Berlin, all they could do was look about the encircling states, and be grateful for their little enclave of freedom.

Before the wall, aspirant refugees from all over East Germany made their way to East Berlin intending to continue their journey over to the western part of the city. After the wall, although East Berliners continued to venture to the West, Berlin was no longer the magnet it had been. Those who sought to go west gravitated now to other parts of East Germany, where the barriers were less intensely guarded.

One family used a homemade balloon for a twenty-eight-minute flight across the East–West border to Upper Franconia. Munich attorney Heinz Heidrich hired Barry

Meeker, a decorated Vietnam War veteran, to fly his clients to the Free World in a helicopter. Meeker gave a wry tribute to the complicated machine he had used in Vietnam: "I thought, 'Here's a really good thing to do with a helicopter.'" A symphony orchestra percussionist was permitted from time to time to tour abroad, but his wife had to stay home as hostage. Finally, the percussionist fitted her into a kettledrum, and over she went to the West.

Herr Heidrich also used horses to get people out of East Germany—not by mounting the refugees on horseback, but by creating a horse van with a hidden compartment that would hold five people, no less. Of course, for verisimilitude, he had to transport real horses along with his real refugees. "What those horses cost!" he complained to the American journalist Peter Wyden. (Unlike Fuchs and Spina and other early saints of the movement, these second-generation escape helpers charged expenses plus; $10,000 to $12,000 was considered reasonable, and some charged considerably more.)

In the early days of the wall there were frequent scenes of painfully distant reunions, many of them captured on film, since the wall and its implications never ceased to be a magnet for photographers. A daughter hands her mother flowers across the barbed wire, wishing her a happy birthday. Wedding parties gather near low places in the wall to wave to their separated families. A West Berlin woman climbs up a ladder, helped by her husband and young daughter, to show the face of her new baby to relatives in the East. Whole buildingsful of people, some with binoculars, wave handkerchiefs at the windows in the buildings opposite, whose inhabitants wave back.

But even such attenuated intimacies became more difficult and eventually impossible as the wall grew to thirteen
feet tall, with a death strip and a second wall behind it.
And then, once it was permitted (though it was never easy
or cheap) for West Berliners to travel to the East for real
reunions, the long-distance trysts faded out. But a different sort of reunion persisted, as simple crosses were placed
near the wall, with flowers and wreaths frequently
renewed, in memory of those who had tried to come over
and failed.

On October 21, 1969, Willy Brandt finally took the prize
he had been seeking the night the border was closed: he
was now chancellor of West Germany. His political victory
didn't bespeak a dramatic shift in voting patterns since the
previous election. The Christian Democratic Union and its
Bavarian sister party, the Christian Social Union, led by the
doughty conservative Franz-Josef Strauss, took 46.1 percent of the vote, down narrowly from their 47.6 in 1965.
The Social Democrats took 42.7 percent (up from 39.3).
The difference came from a shift in loyalty of the small
Free Democratic Party (FPD).

In 1966 the Free Democrats had precipitated a government crisis by withdrawing from the CDU/CSU coalition.
This had led to the formation of the so-called Grand Coalition: the CDU/CSU under Kurt Georg Kiesinger, and the
SPD under Brandt. Now, after the 1969 elections, the FPD
declared its willingness to form a government with the SPD.

Thus Brandt became the first Social Democratic chancellor in postwar German history. He was now free to go

full bore on his Ostpolitik (East-oriented politics), which he had tentatively launched as foreign minister in the Kiesinger government. Ostpolitik was the brainchild of Brandt's longtime associate Egon Bahr, who had first floated the concept in a speech in 1963.

Bahr had had a brief taste of life in East Germany. At the end of World War II, his neighborhood had wound up in the Soviet Sector of Berlin. He stayed on for a while, scrounging about for work as a freelance investigative reporter. He soon found that the last thing the new rulers of East Germany wanted was accurate reporting, and he left for West Berlin in 1946. Now, in the 1960s, he enunciated a policy for West Germany based on the realities as he saw them. There were now two Germanies, like it or not. For West Germany to refuse to acknowledge East Germany as a separate polity, he believed, was simply self-indulgent nostalgia. Moreover, the problems of ordinary Germans on both sides of the border could be much better addressed by negotiating than by stonewalling.

Adenauer's Christian Democrats did not ignore the de facto realities of life. But just as the Nationalist Chinese in Taiwan refused formal relations with Communist China, so, Adenauer maintained, West Germany should not deal formally with East Germany. To negotiate with the GDR, to sign treaties, would undercut Bonn's position as the legitimate authority over the entire country.

By 1968 Adenauer was dead and Brandt had a cabinet post in the Grand Coalition government. Bahr was now able to put out cautious feelers toward the East. Richard Nixon sent out a feeler of his own during his visit to Berlin in February 1969, a month after his inauguration as president. Soviet foreign minister Andrei Gromyko tentatively responded. Gromyko was looking for ways to minimize problems on the Soviet Union's western flank, in order to give greater attention to what Moscow viewed as a developing Chinese menace.

These feelers eventually led, in March 1970, to negotiations among the four occupying powers designed to "normalize" living conditions for citizens of Berlin. These negotiations frequently stalled, and in January 1971 Bahr flew to Washington to meet with Henry Kissinger and solicit his help. Kissinger had strong reservations about Bahr's Ostpolitik, which seemed to legitimize the division of Europe. But Kissinger accepted the proposition that something needed to be done to ease the strains on the daily lives of Berliners, and he endorsed the negotiations.

The Quadripartite Agreement was finally signed on September 3, 1971. Among the immediate results, the GDR would no longer hinder traffic between West Germany and West Berlin. Direct-dial phone service would be introduced within "the relevant area" (that was the name given in the agreement to Berlin). Permission, subject to fees and credentials, for West Berliners to visit East Berlin, granted fitfully since 1963, would be made permanent. Further negotiations would lead, by the end of 1972, to a formal treaty between the two Germanies in which each recognized the other as a sovereign and independent state.

The four-power negotiations on Berlin overlapped with Kissinger's top-secret preparations for Nixon's trip to China. The parallel was there: diplomatic steps to acknowledge realities.

·   ·   ·

In April 1968, East German citizens were allowed to vote on a new constitution, which they approved, in true Bolshevik style, by 94.54 percent. The new document, replacing the 1949 constitution, brought the Eastern Zone's law into line with its practice. The rights to strike, to demonstrate, to emigrate, granted in the earlier constitution as exhibitionistic human-rights festoonery, were revoked. Freedom of the press, which had never been practiced, was formally nullified. The Socialist Unity Party was formally recognized as the only legal party in the German Democratic Republic. Any steps toward unification of the two Germanies could be taken "only on the basis of democracy and socialism." The new constitution was the high-water mark for Walter Ulbricht, who would be the principal casualty of Ostpolitik.

Ulbricht had been the de facto head of the East German government almost from the moment he rode back into Berlin with Marshal Zhukov in 1945. Immediately after the war, he helped to engineer the merger of the Communist Party, under Wilhelm Pieck, with the Social Democratic Party, under Otto Grotewohl, to form the Socialist Unity Party. Ulbricht was junior both to Pieck, who became the president of the new German Democratic Republic in 1949, and to Grotewohl, who became premier. But Ulbricht was Moscow's man, and it was he, not his technical superiors, who regularly visited the Kremlin to advise on German policy. In 1950 he was made secretary-general of the Socialist Unity Party.

Now, in May 1971, the true believer foundered on the rocks of détente. Because he resisted rapprochement with the West, the Kremlin decided to replace him. But he was let down gently, by comparison with many Eastern Bloc leaders who had proved unsatisfactory to Moscow. Although he resigned as secretary-general of the Party, he was allowed to remain actively involved in the government, as chairman of the Council of State. He would die of a stroke in 1973, at age eighty.

And of course his successor met all the qualifications. Erich Honecker, age fifty-eight, was a true believer too, the son of a Communist and a Communist himself from age ten, a man "treasured by the entire Party," as Ulbricht put it in his retirement speech. Honecker, however, lacked his mentor's inflexible sense of rectitude. If Moscow wanted détente and "normalization" in Eastern Europe, Honecker would not lie awake nights worrying about deviationism.

On October 20, 1971, Willy Brandt was awarded the Nobel Peace Prize for his "concrete initiatives leading to the relaxation of tension" between East and West. The prize did not bring serenity. Two years later Brandt's political life fell apart with the revelation that one of his chief aides, Günther Guillaume, was a Communist spy.

Guillaume was a teenager when the war came to an end, living in what would soon become the Soviet Sector of Berlin. His first real job was as a low-level editor with Volk und Welt, the semiofficial publishing house of the East German government. In the late 1940s he was approached by the HVA (Hauptverwaltung Aufklärung), the foreign-intelligence division of the Stasi. He would serve under the legendary spymaster Markus Wolf.

Guillaume was sent for training to a school in Kiev founded by Comrade Beria himself. When he returned to Berlin, he was ordered to marry another member of the HVA, Christel Boom. In 1956 the couple was sent to Frankfurt as agents in place, with instructions to infiltrate and report on the activity of the Social Democratic Party.

The Guillaumes proved able and extraordinarily resourceful. With Wolf's encouragement, Günther rose in the ranks of the local SPD. In the 1969 federal election, he served as campaign manager for Georg Leber, an elderly trade-union official who had been minister for transport in Chancellor Kiesinger's Grand Coalition. When that election resulted in Brandt's coming to power, Leber strongly recommended Günther Guillaume for a post in the new government.

Some questions were raised about Guillaume's past, but he answered them satisfactorily—Brandt's people had no stomach for Red-hunting. Guillaume rose quickly to become one of Brandt's top assistants. The intimacy between the two men went beyond office work. Guillaume often traveled with the chancellor and sometimes went with the Brandts on family vacations, bringing along Christel and their son, Pierre.

Guillaume soon had unlimited access to NATO secrets, including information on nuclear weapons in Europe, Allied contingency plans for meeting a Warsaw Pact attack, interrogation protocols for refugee camps, and Western negotiating positions in the four-power talks on Berlin. It was often he who retrieved messages from Brandt's personal telex; he once netted some unbuttoned comments by President Nixon on the stance of the French government.

Guillaume's information was of such high quality that KGB chief Yuri Andropov frequently sent copies of his raw reports to Gromyko, to give him the full flavor of Guillaume's achievements.

It wasn't until May 1973 that West German intelligence caught on to the Guillaumes. Accosted with the evidence, Brandt was for a while in hot and wide-eyed denial. But the BND (Bundesnachrichtendienst, the West German intelligence agency) had a strong enough case that Brandt finally had to submit. The BND requested him to keep Guillaume on staff until further notice, intending to pass on disinformation to East Berlin and Moscow, and to accumulate further evidence to present, in due course, to a West German court. Brandt agreed to play along, and the deception went on for eleven months, sorely testing Mr. Brandt's theatrical resources.

At 6:30 A.M. on April 24, 1974, there was a knock on the door of the Guillaumes' apartment and eighteen-year-old Pierre went to answer it, thinking it was the usual morning delivery from the bakery. Instead, it was four policemen. Pierre called out to his father, who came to the door. The police told Günther he was under arrest for espionage. Ignoring all his training (apprehended agents, much like prisoners of war, are supposed to recite only their name, address, and date of birth), he declaimed: "I am an officer of the National People's Army of the GDR and a member of the Ministry for State Security. I beseech you to respect my honor as an officer." Why he did this, he never explained; his boss, Markus Wolf, speculates that he wanted to cut a dashing figure before his son, who was going through a teenage rebellion. In any case, it was a

godsend to the West German police, whose case had not
been airtight.

The scandal was the main topic in West Germany for
weeks—and not entirely at the geopolitical level. There were
rumors that Guillaume, a dedicated womanizer, had sometimes made arrangements for his boss, similarly inclined. On
May 6, Brandt went on television to announce that he was
resigning "out of respect for the unwritten rules of democracy and also to prevent my political and personal integrity
from being destroyed." But it was not until July 1975 that
Günther and Christel Guillaume were put on trial in Düs-
seldorf, with a rueful former chancellor testifying for the
prosecution. On December 15, 1975, Günther was convicted of high treason and sentenced to thirteen years in
prison; Christel was convicted of treason and complicity in
espionage and sentenced to eight years.

At the time of their sentencing, a West German government spokesman announced that the Guillaumes were too
potentially dangerous to be repatriated in exchange for
Westerners held in East German prisons. However, by
1981 the danger was judged to have passed, and they were
exchanged (Christel in March, Günther in October) for
fourteen assorted spies and political prisoners.

Günther was in poor health. He "had been out of the
game too long" to be of much further use, Wolf commented in his memoirs. And the Guillaumes' marriage,
rocky before their arrest, had not survived the separation.
The Stasi gave Günther a nice house in the countryside
from which he commuted into Berlin three times a week
to lecture at the Stasi espionage school. He died in 1995,
at age sixty-eight.

Brandt had become president of the Socialist International, a post he held until his death in 1992 at age seventy-eight.

Ever since August 16, 1961, the East Germans had worked steadily to improve the "anti-fascist protective rampart," their official term for the wall. There was, starting that first week, the replacement of barbed wire with concrete, followed by the construction of watchtowers. By the end of 1961, the watchtowers numbered 130. Five years later there were 210 of them; by 1989 there were 297. Where the view from a watchtower was thought unsatisfactory, guard dogs were put in on long leads, ready to assault any refugee who got that far. The death strip was gradually extended until it was two hundred yards wide in places. By the time I first visited Berlin, in 1970, starting from the Eastern side, the prospective refugee came first to a low wall, about five feet high; then to a trip wire that activated an alarm; then to a section floodlit at night and guarded by Grepos in the watchtowers and by the dogs; and finally to the main wall, about thirteen feet high. In 1976, when the wall was fifteen years old, the Honecker government decided on a complete overhaul. The original rough-cast concrete was gradually replaced with smooth concrete slabs, and the barbed wire along the top was replaced with concrete pipe, resembling drainage pipe, a foot or so in diameter. In fact, the pipe protruded a couple of inches on either side of the wall, making it even harder than before for a climber to gain a handhold on the top. Only in the heavily guarded area right in front of the Brandenburg Gate did the wall have a flat top, about ten feet wide, thus permitting guards to stand there, symbols of armed adamance.

One unforeseen result of the reconstruction was that the new smooth concrete provided a perfect surface for graffitists. Before long, virtually every square inch of the Western side of the wall was covered with drawings and text and symbols. The Eastern side remained pristine, cement-white. Some of the graffiti were obscene, many were banal; a few were witty, some prophetic ("This wall must go." "Will the last one out switch off the light?"). There were paintings, including disquieting scenes with monsters and skulls. Viewing platforms were built on the Western side, and the wall became a major tourist attraction, visited by thousands each day.

Opinions differed on the seemliness of this. To some critics it was like bear-baiting—profiting from misery. "Should this really be a tourist attraction?" asked one woman interviewed by West German radio. "I don't think it's a good idea." For others, it was profoundly educational, the Iron Curtain in concrete, shockingly illuminating the nature of the Communist enterprise. As the French painter Michel Butor put it, "You must have *touched* the wall itself to comprehend that it is real."

To West Berliners, the wall became a fact of life. One man whose garden was bounded by the wall was interviewed by West German television in 1981, on the twentieth anniversary. We see him turning sausages on the grill as friends and family lounge comfortably around a table, twenty feet from the wall. "With time you get used to the wall," the man tells us. "You've got to deal with it as best you can. . . . After a while, you can even forget it's there."

But then there are times like an evening the previous November, when three people tried to come over the wall into his garden. Two made it; the third, a young woman, was shot to death. Her friends "hung a wreath in my garden, in her memory," the man relates. "When something happens at the wall, something like this attempted escape last fall, then you wake up and realize what this is really all about."

The Eastern Bloc under Leonid Brezhnev seemed as dispiritingly solid as ever. It was as if the whole of the Iron Curtain, from the Black Sea to the Baltic Sea, were one great Berlin Wall. Even when the Soviet Union signed the Helsinki Accords in 1975, which mandated freedom of movement and of ideas, no one was under any illusion that the Kremlin actually intended to permit freedom of movement and of public expression.

But there *were* changes. Dubcek, in 1968, did not suffer the fate of Jan Masaryk in 1948. Dubcek's punishment was quaint. Preferred to the defenestration of Masaryk, but oddly condescending. He was permitted to live. And to work, under observation, as a forestry official in his native Slovakia. Solzhenitsyn and Bukovsky and Sakharov, in the 1970s, did not suffer the fate of Osip Mandelstam in the 1930s or of Imre Nagy in the 1950s; they were dispatched, unwilling, into exile, external or internal; but they did not disappear, were not shot.

In Hungary Janos Kadar, put in power by Khrushchev in 1956 to finish cleaning up after the rebellion, began, in the Sixties, to ease up on speech codes. His government put increasing emphasis on consumer goods, in what came to be known as "goulash Communism."

In Poland in 1970, protests against a sharp increase in food prices were in fact brutally crushed, with an official toll of forty-five dead. But there was a price to pay. Party leader Wladyslaw Gomulka was forced to resign, in favor of the more latitudinarian Edward Gierek.

In 1977 there was a major breach in the Communist modus vivendi. It happened, once again, in Czechoslovakia. This time it was not the government, as in the Prague Spring, but a group of private citizens. They began by collecting 241 signatures on what they called Charter 77. This was a samizdat document listing, in about three thousand words, the ways in which the government of Gustav Husak was violating the human rights that had been guaranteed by Helsinki. The signers—they were called Chartari (Chartists)—pledged to work toward obtaining those rights for all Czechoslovakians. Many of the Chartists were well-known artists and writers, but there were also parish priests, computer programmers, civil servants, manual laborers, and a famous widow, Josefa Slanska: her "Titoist, cosmopolitan" husband, Rudolf Slansky, had been hanged after a show trial in Prague in 1952.

The Husak regime's reaction to Charter 77 was sharp but cautious. Prague denounced the document as "slanderous" and "demagogic" and condemned the signers as "adventurers," "shipwreckers," and "self-appointed elitists." But—the government exacted prison terms rather than using the firing squad or the gallows as discipline.

Despite the regime's attacks, Charter 77 kept circulating underground. By its first anniversary, it had acquired

932 signers. Most of them were imprisoned, if only briefly—notably Vaclav Havel and his fellow playwright Pavel Kohout. The Czech-British playwright Tom Stoppard celebrated them and the Charter movement in a brilliant one-act play, *Cahoot's Macbeth*.

The Chartists were eager to encourage emerging dissidents in neighboring Poland. During 1977–1978, clandestine meetings were held at several points along the border. Polish protesters were also encouraged by the Catholic Church. In September 1978 every Polish bishop signed a letter describing censorship as "a weapon of totalitarian regimes" and calling for "openness and free public opinion." The following year, Poland was visited by her illustrious native son Pope John Paul II.

At the same time as these calls for political freedom were going forward, Polish workers were growing bolder in protesting the economic failures of Communism. There was agitation for better working conditions and for free (i.e., non-Communist) trade unions. The principal agitator was an out-of-work electrician (he had been fired for political reasons) named Lech Walesa, who leapt to national and international hero status during a strike at the Gdansk shipyard in August 1980. In September, as strikes spread throughout Poland, Gierek was ousted as Party leader on the grounds that his failed policies had led to the labor unrest. In October the regime recognized Walesa's national union, which he called Solidarity.

When the strikes nonetheless continued in full force, the Soviets wheeled twenty-six divisions up to the Soviet–Polish border. To forestall an invasion, the Polish CP Central Committee dismissed the premier, Josef

Pinkowski, in February 1981, replacing him with Defense Minister Wojciech Jaruzelski.

Jaruzelski was considered a moderate. He was a member of the group that had toppled Gomulka in 1970, and in 1976 he told his Politburo colleagues that he would never use the army against a workers' demonstration: "Polish soldiers will not fire on Polish workers."

At first the reformers welcomed the appointment of Jaruzelski. Walesa described him as "our last chance." But when there was no substantive improvement in working conditions, the strikes started up again and continued throughout the summer.

On December 12, Solidarity called for a national referendum on four questions. Two of them read, "Should a temporary government be established and free elections held?" and "Should Poland's military alliance with the Soviet Union be supported?" Moscow had already said it straight out: If Warsaw didn't take "radical steps" to control the country, the Soviet troops massed on the border would march in. And so it was the "moderate," Jaruzelski, who imposed martial law on December 13, 1981. He called it Operation Springtime, a Polish joke. All the civil liberties that had been won over the previous four years were suspended, censorship was imposed, and thousands of Solidarity members were arrested, beginning with Lech Walesa. But a reprise of Hungary 1956 or Czechoslovakia 1968 had been averted.

Ronald Reagan had been elected president just a year before. He condemned the Polish repression, as Presidents

Eisenhower and Johnson had condemned the repressions directly imposed by the Soviets in 1956 and 1968. However, Reagan didn't let it go at that. Under his auspices and at his direction, the planted axioms of the Cold War were fetched up and challenged. What ensued were studies evolving into a series of "national security decision directives." Key of these was NSDD-75, issued in December 1982. Reagan's national security adviser William Clark summarized the meaning of NSDD-75. For a long time, Clark explained, the United States had had a policy of "external resistance to Soviet imperialism" and negotiation "to eliminate, on the basis of strict reciprocity, outstanding disagreements." That would continue, but the directive also called for something new: stimulating "internal pressure on the USSR to weaken the sources of Soviet imperialism."

It was slow work, consuming the rest of Reagan's time in office. But it made way for the end of the Cold War.

In 1986 the wall turned twenty-five, prompting great media attention. In West Germany, refugees and veteran escape helpers were interviewed, their sentiments broadcast. Rainer Hildebrandt, the founder and curator of the Checkpoint Charlie Museum, invited American graffitist Keith Haring to paint something appropriate on the wall. He did: a large mural of anxious Germans, arms upraised against the impossibility of scaling the wall, while one of their number has found a ladder and is climbing up it. The artist supplied a caption, written in English: "happy birthday."

Seeking East German comment on the anniversary, the American journalist Peter Wyden got through to several high-ranking officials. He expected to find them defensive about the wall. Not at all. They were unanimous in acclaiming it as a brilliant accomplishment. One of Wyden's sources bubbled with enthusiasm: "August 13, 1961! That was the basic breakthrough! The wall was our graduation exam!" Another was no less delighted but more analytical: "It was a worthwhile investment. Finally we [got] clarity. The wall made normalization possible."

On the anniversary day itself, the East Germans held a parade, and West Germans made speeches denouncing the wall. The British journalist Anthony Kemp summed up the anniversary with a fatalistic opinion generally accepted as realistic. He wrote, "The probability is that [the wall] will still be there for the 50th anniversary."

One man was less than fatalistic. Ronald Reagan had first viewed the wall as a private citizen in 1978. "We have got to find a way to knock this thing down," he told his traveling companions, future national security adviser Dick Allen and aide Peter Hannaford. As president, Reagan went again to Berlin in 1982. He outraged Eastern sensibilities by committing a Grenzverletzung, a border injury: he took a couple of ceremonial steps across the painted border line at Checkpoint Charlie, without the express permission demanded.

In June 1987, Reagan returned to Berlin. The occasion was the 750th anniversary of the city's founding, and he had been invited to speak at an outdoor ceremony. Some

European commentators observed that Berlin was a young city compared with Athens, Rome, Paris, London, Toledo, and a dozen others. Reagan failed to make a joke on the question whether he or Berlin had been born first, but he did better.

He had, by the time of this visit, twice met with Mikhail Gorbachev, and their meetings were friendly. Gorbachev's espousal of glasnost—candor in speech—and perestroika—the restructuring of the economy—were more in the way of declarations than policies. But they were landmarks, and Reagan would make the most of them.

The site was the plaza across the wall from the Brandenburg Gate. This time, in contrast with Kennedy's visit twenty-four years earlier, there were no red banners blocking the president's view up Unter den Linden. There was a slightly incongruous pane of glass between the lectern and the Brandenburg Gate—bulletproof glass, installed to thwart any assassination attempt. On this warm but overcast June day, the plaza was packed with thousands waving miniature American and West German flags.

Flanked by Chancellor Helmut Kohl and by Philip Jenninger, president of the West German parliament, Reagan rose to speak. He recapped the devastation of Germany in 1945 and the miraculous rebuilding of the Western portion of the country, accomplished with the help of its former enemy, through the Marshall Plan.

Reagan now addressed the Soviet leader directly: "General Secretary Gorbachev, if you seek peace, if you seek prosperity for the Soviet Union and Eastern Europe, if you seek liberalization, come here to this gate. *Mr. Gorbachev, open this gate. Mr. Gorbachev, tear down this wall.*" The crowd went wild.

It was much later that historians learned how close some members of the administration had come to suppressing those electric lines, the most renowned of Reagan's presidency. The draft of the speech had come out of the speechwriting shop and was sent routinely to the State Department and the National Security Council for vetting. Red flags shot up. The president must not speak those words. They would harm Gorbachev and get in the way of continuing Soviet reforms. And if Reagan used such language, it would harm *him*. Any demand so importunate, so outrageous and inflammatory, was among other things "not presidential." But one or two of the president's aides made the point that it was up to him to decide whether those words were presidential. Reagan's decision lives in history—in Berlin, of course, and worldwide.

4

The Wall Came Tumbling Down

A generation had elapsed between "Ich bin ein Berliner" and "Mr. Gorbachev, tear down this wall." One year and a half after Reagan made his mythogenic plea, he left office, and the wall was still standing. The day before George H. W. Bush's inauguration, Erich Honecker reaffirmed his commitment to the wall. Outgoing secretary of state George Shultz had designated the wall as the "acid test" of Eastern Europe's progress toward human rights. Honecker defiantly replied: "It will stand in fifty or a hundred years."

Bravado notwithstanding, the Iron Curtain was fraying. In the spring of 1988, Janos Kadar had been forced to resign as general secretary of the Hungarian Socialist Workers' (i.e., Communist) Party, although he had sponsored liberal reforms. The new general secretary, Karoly Grosz, shot ahead, permitting opposition groups to operate openly and exploring the possibility of multiparty elections.

In November 1988, Margaret Thatcher visited Warsaw. Poland was still under martial law, and Solidarity still illegal. When Mrs. Thatcher, at a state dinner, called for "personal and political liberty" as the only way to solve Poland's economic problems, President Jaruzelski reacted sharply. "Words," he said, "are the cheapest goods on the world market." But his representatives were already meeting with Lech Walesa and other Solidarity leaders.

In East Germany itself, there was little liberalization and little popular ferment. To be sure, there were traces of moderation. In November 1987, the regime rescinded the Grepos' shoot-to-kill orders (orders the regime had denied were ever issued). But there was nothing in the way of organic reform—Honecker scorned perestroika, insisting that it would be counterproductive in the Democratic Republic of Germany.

As for the citizens of East Germany, they made do with what was called "nightly emigration." West German television broadcasts could be seen nearly everywhere in the GDR, giving viewers a familiarity with Western news, habits, and diversions that was almost unique behind the Iron Curtain. But vicarious participation in the affairs of the West served as a political sedative rather than a stimulant. Honecker's citizenry remained among the most docile in the satellite world, more like the servile Bulgaria and Romania than like the restive Poland, Hungary, and Czechoslovakia.

While Moscow's Eastern European empire destabilized, Gorbachev had plenty to worry about at home. He had known when he came to power, in March 1985, that he was inheriting an economy that was no better off than it had been twenty-one years before, when Khrushchev was ousted. Gorbachev was also inheriting the Soviet occupation of Afghanistan. Casualties there were heavy, and popular morale was eroding.

The Reagan administration's efforts under NSDD-75 to develop an anti-missile program had been scoffed at—"Star Wars" was not a friendly nickname. But the program had been launched, and Gorbachev was hard-pressed. He couldn't simply ignore it. So he took it on with his own anti-missile defense program, in what quickly became a huge state enterprise, threatening to bankrupt the Union of Soviet Socialist Republics. In December 1987 he signed the Intermediate-Range Nuclear Forces (INF) treaty with Reagan, an effort at cutting the costs of the arms race. In the last year of the Reagan administration, Gorbachev attempted to capitalize on the relaxations generated by that treaty, calling for a "common European home."

At a state dinner in Yugoslavia in March 1988, he laid out his vision of a new Europe: "I have said it once and I will say it again. We are interested in eliminating the divisions of Europe. What we need is an honest and effective policy of good-neighborliness. . . . Economic alliances and cooperation and the gradual advancement toward a common European market are the vital prerequisites for the peaceful future of Europe." (Mrs. Thatcher would reply on her visit to Warsaw eight months later, nicely exploiting the wall: "President Gorbachev had spoken of building a common European house. But the only wall so far erected is the Berlin Wall, which divides and separates.")

On top of his other problems, Gorbachev faced outbreaks of nationalism within the Soviet Union itself. In
June 1988, Christian Armenians living in Nagorno-
Karabakh, an enclave within the Muslim-dominated Azer-
baizhani Republic, complained to the Kremlin of ill
treatment by the local government. The adjoining Arme-
nian Republic proposed nothing less than an annexation of
the enclave. This was the very first time, Western observers
clucked, that there had been an open territorial dispute
between two Soviet republics. But it was only the first of
many unprecedented events that summer. A month later in
Lithuania, a group calling itself the Initiative Group in
Support of Perestroika held a rally at which speakers
called, no less, for a popular referendum in Nagorno-
Karabakh. The People's Front of Estonia, a nationalist
political group, was suddenly accorded official recognition
by the Estonian Republic, with Moscow's tacit acceptance.
And in the third of the Baltic nations, Latvia, the writers'
union asked that the republic be declared a "sovereign
state." Never mind the paradox, a sovereign state within a
sovereign state: it was the first time an official organization
in a Soviet republic had made such a licentious call. As the
dispute between the Armenians and the Azerbaizhanis
erupted into violent clashes, the Supreme Soviet approved
a decree giving the security forces broad authority to suppress demonstrations and to arrest suspected agitators.
There was nothing unexpected in the decree itself. But it
was breathtaking to learn that thirty-one members of the
1,500-man Supreme Soviet had voted nay and twenty-six
had abstained. This was the first time that a decree of that
body was other than unanimous.

In May, Gorbachev had announced that a special Party conference would take place the following month. On June 28 the All-Union Conference of the Soviet Communist Party convened in Moscow, the first such conference with representatives from every part of the country since 1941. Gorbachev's 3½-hour opening address ranged from his program for economic reform to the need for religious freedom and equality for women. But the most striking passage was his call for a radical restructuring of the central government, with a strong president and a Congress of People's Deputies. Gorbachev declared: "The people demand total democracy, full-blooded democracy with no reservations. There can be no compromise." Granted, by "democracy" he didn't mean anything recognizable as that in the West. Only the Communist Party would be permitted to participate in elections, Gorbachev explained, and only Party members would be eligible to run for the new Congress. "A multiparty system—two parties, three parties—it is all rubbish," he would later tell a Kremlin gathering. "At first [it is] 1 or 2 parties on class grounds, then 120 on national grounds, then international. All that is thrown at us by irresponsible people." But there was progress. His plan called for 1,500 of the Congress's 2,250 seats to be filled through secret-ballot voting by ordinary citizens; the rest of the deputies would be appointed by local trade unions and Party organizations. None of them would be appointed by the Kremlin.

The enthusiasm of Gorbachev's colleagues, at home and in Eastern Europe, was not unqualified. Of the satellite regimes, Hungary alone responded positively. The GDR's news agency concentrated on the economic aspects of the speech, arguing that Gorbachev had nothing to teach East Germany, whose economy was the healthiest in the Eastern Bloc. Yes, but an ice age behind West Germany's.

In December 1988, the Supreme Soviet voted to go ahead with this stage of Gorbachev's perestroika.

Through the spring of 1989, the Polish and Hungarian regimes seemed to be in a suicidal race to be the first to topple. On February 11, the Central Committee of Hungary's Socialist Workers' Party approved in principle the legalization of independent political parties. What would this actually mean? Would the new parties be independent as in France, Britain, Italy, and West Germany? Or independent as in Czechoslovakia? There they were separate from the ruling party, but not free to oppose it. General Secretary Grosz was ambiguous, and the draft of a new Hungarian constitution, submitted to parliament on March 8, echoed his ambiguity. It provided for a multiparty system but stated that Hungary would continue as a "socialist" country and as a "people's republic." But there were symbolic concessions of resonant meaning. The Party decided to remove the red star from Hungary's flag and replace it with the Crown of St. Stephen. Blue-collar workers were permitted to form Hungary's first independent trade union, which, with a nod to their Polish counterparts, they dubbed the Solidarity Workers' Trade Union Federation. At the beginning of April, the opposition, led by a group called the Democratic Forum, agreed to enter power-sharing discussions with the government.

In Poland, the Solidarity Party was legalized on April

17. On June 4, Poland held its first free elections since 1935. Solidarity won a smashing 99 of the 100 seats in the new Senate, and all the open seats in the lower house, the Sejm. (Under the rules set by the Jaruzelski regime, 299 seats in the Sejm were reserved for the United Workers' [i.e., Communist] Party and its allies, while 161 were open to other parties.)

Jaruzelski pleaded with Solidarity to join the Communists in a new ruling coalition. At first Walesa refused. Then he proposed a coalition, but hardly what Jaruzelski had in mind: Solidarity would be the senior partner and the Communists the junior partner. On August 17, Jaruzelski became the first leader in the satellite world to preside over the transfer of power to a non-Communist government.

On August 20, at a Mass at St. Brygida's in Gdansk, the church nearest the shipyard where Solidarity had begun, the choir and congregation joined in singing the Polish national hymn, which begins "Poland is not dead while still we live." That hymn had been sung for many bloody years, but sung quietly, Poles singing to themselves through the long partition of their country among Russia, Prussia, and Austria, and then the Nazi occupation, and then the years of Soviet control. Tadeusz Mazowiecki, a Solidarity activist newly elected Poland's first post-Communist premier, echoed the hymn's opening line in his first speech in the new circumstances: "Poland is alive," he stated. Most of his countrymen cheered, though some grumbled at the suggestion that the Communist domination had been equivalent to those past occupations.

There remained the heart-stopping question: Would

Gorbachev assert the Brezhnev Doctrine? Under its provisions, no territory, having once come within the Soviet orbit, could ever leave it. Warsaw braced itself for the Kremlin's reaction. It came from one of Gorbachev's aides, Yevgeny Primakov, addressing a group of American congressmen. The man who would later become prime minister of Russia told the visitors that it was "entirely a matter to be decided by Poland" what kind of government Poland had. The Brezhnev Doctrine had been de facto nullified.

As Eastern Europe started demanding freedom, in West Berlin there was movement toward the left. For much of the postwar period, both pre- and post-wall, the two major parties of West Germany, the Christian Democrats and the Social Democrats, worked together in West Berlin in an almost nonpartisan fashion. Coalition governments were the norm. That arrangement had gone by the boards in the early Eighties, but the city government still had not radically changed—until 1989. In the municipal elections that January, the two major parties finished in virtually a dead heat—37.8 percent for the CDU, down from its record high of 46.4 percent in 1985; for the SPD, 37.3 percent, up from 32.4 percent.

That was bad news for the CDU government in Bonn under longtime chancellor Helmut Kohl. But the biggest news involved the smaller parties. The mainstream-left Free Democratic Party dropped to below the proportional-representation threshold of 5 percent and so could not contribute to any coalition. Meanwhile, the two extremes of the political spectrum had increased their strength. At one end, the Alternative List, a radical Green party, took 11.8 percent of the vote (up from 10.6 percent). At the other end, the Republican Party—extreme right-wing, maybe even neo-Nazi—more than doubled its vote, from 3 percent to 7.5 percent. Its increase in strength was attributed to an animus against the Third World asylum seekers who had begun to show up in West Berlin in some numbers, deliberately ushered there by the East German government, with an interest in destabilizing West Berlin.

There was an impasse for a period. The CDU promised not to form a coalition with the Republicans, and the SPD promised not to form one with the Greens. But as the situation sputtered on, the Social Democrats went back on their promise and brought in the Greens. The SPD's conditions were strict, and revealing: the Greens were required to accept the Western Allies as the sovereign power, accept West Berlin's ties to West Germany, and renounce the use of force to settle internal political disagreements.

The Greens accepted these terms, but that did not stop them from doing what they could to block President Bush's scheduled visit to West Germany in the spring, following NATO's fortieth-anniversary summit in Brussels. The Kohl government's invitation prevailed, and Bush spent two days in Germany. He did not visit Berlin, but he spoke of the city in his main address on East–West relations. "The Cold War," he said, "began with the division of Europe. It can only end when Europe is whole." Specifically, Europe could not be "whole and free" until the Berlin Wall came down.

· · ·

The West Berlin elections had taken place against a background of high-level maneuvering. Chancellor Kohl unexpectedly found himself an ally of Gorbachev on the matter of the Lance missiles based in West Germany. These were battlefield nuclear weapons. Hence, if there was ever occasion to use them, the country on whose soil they were based would suffer not only from the enemy's retaliatory action, but also from the fallout from the Lances' own warheads. As Kohl phrased it, "Because of the range of the short-range missiles, West Germany is more strongly affected than other members of the alliance." One of Kohl's foreign-policy advisers, Volker Ruhe, put it graphically: "The shorter the range, the deader the Germans." The SPD wanted a total ban on these weapons. With federal elections coming up in 1990, this became a popular issue.

Gorbachev was eager to link the question of missile deployment to the ongoing discussion of conventional forces. He was desperately trying to reduce his over-extended empire's expenses without reducing its relative strength. Even before the Conventional Forces in Europe conference reconvened in May 1989, he had ordered a reduction in the number of Soviet troops and tanks in Hungary and East Germany. Western leaders permitted themselves to wonder—Dick Cheney especially, as U.S. secretary of defense—whether Gorbachev could continue on his current path without losing control of his government.

The first session of the Soviet Union's new Congress of People's Deputies opened on May 25, and by Soviet standards it was uproarious. Gorbachev ran unopposed, and prevailed in the vote for the presidency, 95.6 percent to 4.4 percent. But before the vote was taken, he was subjected to two hours of sharp criticism. One deputy wanted to know where Gorbachev got off building a new dacha for himself in the Crimea while urging austerity for others. Another asked what in fact were the results of perestroika and had the changes done more harm than good. Another deplored the fact that Soviet troops had fired on protesters in the Georgian Republic.

The Congress was roiled by the failure of the former Communist Party chief of Moscow, one Boris Yeltsin, to achieve election to the Supreme Soviet. Yeltsin's supporters included the heroic dissident Andrei Sakharov, who had been permitted to return from internal exile in Gorky to take a seat in the Congress. Sakharov accused the regime of rigging the election to keep Yeltsin out. He told a crowd of ten thousand gathered in Moscow's Luzhinsky Park that "the people do not trust the authorities, and the authorities do not trust the people."

Gorbachev had no love for Yeltsin, but he needed to avoid any impression that his new democracy was a farce. When a member of the Supreme Soviet offered to resign in order to provide a seat for Yeltsin, Gorbachev accepted the offer.

On June 12, Gorbachev, with his new title of president, made his first state visit to West Germany. His reception was remarkable. He was hailed by crowds chanting "Gorby! Gorby!" In fact, he was greeted much more warmly than President Bush had been two weeks earlier. A poll recorded 90 percent of West Germans as believing they could trust Gorbachev, as against 58 percent for President Bush and 50 percent for Chancellor Kohl. This was evidence of the strategic restlessness. It was as simple as that the overwhelming majority of West Germans, sensing the true change in Moscow, looked at Gorbachev and saw the possibility of their country's being made whole again.

The shift in passions and the itch of genuine confusion hit the East German rulers hard. The hierarchy in East Berlin had been dismissive of events in Hungary and Poland, and indeed in the Soviet Union itself. Kurt Hager, chief ideologist for the East German Politburo, remarked: "Would you feel bound to repaper the walls of your apartment because your neighbor was repapering his?"

But the effects of Gorbachev's policies could not be brushed aside. Sergei Kondrashev, the former head of the KGB's German operations, was now a special consultant to the new head of the KGB, Vladimir Kryuchkov, a protégé of the late Yuri Andropov. Kondrashev customarily spent a part of his vacation in East Berlin, visiting his old friend Erich Mielke. This time, as Kondrashev later recorded, Mielke asked him, "Sergei, what does Gorbachev think he is doing? If [his] policy with regard to Poland and Hungary continues, the GDR will not be able to contain the social forces" that will be released. Gorbachev must understand this, Mielke warned solemnly. If the Soviet policy is not changed, "the German Democratic Republic will be crushed!" Kondrashev passed this warning on to his boss, Kryuchkov, who passed it on to Gorbachev. When asked what Gorbachev's reaction had been, Kryuchkov reported, "There was none."

On May 2, 1989, the Grosz regime decided to open Hungary's border with (neutral) Austria. The governments of East Germany, Romania, and Czechoslovakia were furious as news came in of Hungarian soldiers methodically cutting and rolling up the barbed wire and the electric fencing that had been strung two decades earlier, replacing the mine fields that had originally separated East from West. Budapest was undeterred—and Moscow didn't step in to halt the opening of this artery.

Andras Kovari, a spokesman for the Hungarian Interior Ministry, gave his reason for the opening: "Not only do we need the world, but the world needs us. An era will be closed with the removal of this fence, and we hope that such systems will never be needed again." He added that he had no reason to believe that many Hungarians would attempt to flee. Why should they? They were, after all, able to travel abroad with few restrictions. But he sought to reassure the Honecker regime by saying that Budapest would not permit a flood of refugees from neighboring countries to use Hungary as a mere passageway, in the manner of East Germans, pre-wall, making their way first to East Berlin and then on through to West Berlin.

But of course there was movement, even if not in the volume feared by the GDR. Between early May and the end of July, several hundred East Germans went to Hungary, ostensibly simply as vacationers, and then crossed over into Austria. Another five hundred were caught trying to cross over and sent home with a stamp on their passports indicating that they had attempted to flee.

The most enterprising escape was via the border town of Sopron. A Hungarian–Austrian "friendship picnic" was scheduled for August 19. As soon as the border guards opened a gate to let the Austrian picnickers into Hungary,

East Germans waiting nearby rushed through the gate, into Austria. Some nine hundred Germans crossed over, believed to be the largest number to escape on any single day.

The westbound passion, once revived, seemed irrepressible. Aspirant East German refugees got the idea of taking physical refuge on West German diplomatic property. This happened first at the embassy in Budapest, then at the embassies in Prague and Warsaw, then at the diplomatic mission in East Berlin itself, established when the two Germanies recognized each other in 1972. Bonn, panicked at the thought of provocations that would threaten the desired movement going on within the Soviet Bloc, ordered locked the gates to all its embassies and missions. So what did the East Germans do? Many of them, showing entrepreneurial determination, climbed over the iron fences surrounding the embassy grounds—one more wall.

On August 3, a Hungarian official told a radio interviewer that the government was considering giving asylum to East Germans on a case-by-case basis. Over the Labor Day weekend, we in America saw on our television screens footage of East Germans milling about in rain-soaked refugee camps, hoping to win favorable attention. The following week, in an interview in the West German magazine *Stern,* the Hungarian interior minister, Istvan Horvath, threw cold water on the whole idea. He announced that Hungary would not permit the passage of refugees until East and West Germany came to an agreement on the question. Even if negotiations went smoothly, it was expected that such an agreement could not be arrived at in less than six weeks, an interminable delay for refugees crowded up against walls and embassy gates and barbed wire, pleading for relief.

The Czechoslovakian government in turn announced that it would not permit the 150-odd East Germans encamped at the West German embassy in Prague to proceed west. "We wouldn't do anything," a spokesman said, to open "a channel of communication that would enable East Germans to leave for West Germany."

Then on September 10, Hungarian foreign minister Gyula Horn announced that the situation had become "unbearable." Budapest would now suspend a twenty-year-old agreement with East Berlin and would permit those East Germans who had made their way onto Hungarian territory to proceed to "a country of their choice." Around thirteen thousand did so over the next four days, some in their own cars, which they had driven into Hungary on their vacations, others on standing-room-only trains.

There were fifty thousand more East German vacationers still loose in Hungary, and it was assumed that at least some of them would press on to the West unless prevented. The Honecker regime protested forcefully, describing Hungary's action as "a clear violation of legal treaties . . . a violation of the basic interests of East Germany." Soviet hard-liner Yegor Ligachev echoed that description. But the incident gave the West a window into the growing strains within the Kremlin, as Soviet Foreign Ministry spokesman Gennady Gerasimov expressed a very different view. Budapest, Gerasimov said, had taken "an unusual step and a very unexpected one . . . naturally this is of some concern to us, but it does not directly affect us." The threat of Soviet intervention seemed now to be remote.

Meanwhile, the negotiations between East and West Germany were indeed proceeding, as Horvath had said. On September 30, West German foreign minister Hans-Dietrich Genscher went to Prague to divulge the results of those negotiations. It was eleven weeks since the first East Germans had taken refuge on the embassy grounds, and by now a total of fifty-five hundred had crowded in. They had been sleeping on the lawns and in a handful of tents; there were long lines for the few toilets and showers.

Genscher elected to deliver his message from the embassy balcony, addressing the thousands waiting anxiously on the lawn below. He was not able to complete the critical sentence. As soon as the refugees understood where he was heading, understood that he was telling them they would be permitted to go to the West, a sustained cheer drowned him out. The next day, the first "freedom train," with passengers hanging out of every window and waving to the TV cameras, left Prague for West Germany. It was an irony that some of these trains were provided by the East German government, and made their way through a corner of East German territory. The Honecker regime covered itself by describing the exodus not as a flight of Germans seeking a freer life, but as an expulsion by East Germany of "irresponsible anti-social traitors and criminals." But the regime also nailed shut the two-hundred-mile-long border between East Germany and Czechoslovakia, which had for years been almost as open as the border between the United States and Canada. One up in the war against traitors and criminals!

Some East Germans, enlivened by events in other satellite nations, formed a group they called the New Forum.

They met initially in Lutheran churches (which had been allowed to stay open notwithstanding East Germany's restrictions on religious practice), notably the St. Nicholas Church in Leipzig and the Gethsemane Church in East Berlin. At first, the New Forum meetings, which included candlelight prayer services, were quiet and moving affairs. Then on September 18, the Monday evening prayer service in Leipzig spilled out into a full-scale march. The same thing happened the next Monday evening, with three times as many people.

The marches spread to other cities, including East Berlin. Participants began carrying homemade banners. A popular slogan called for freedom to travel: Reisenfreiheit. The marchers were frequently attacked by bands of Stasi, dressed in casual trousers and short jackets, looking like young street fighters rather than secret-police officers. They would drag a few of the marchers away and wrench the banners from them, but the proliferation defied the restrictions. Thousands were arrested in that frantic autumn, but soon the marchers began to fight back, and as they marched, they shouted, "Stasi raus! Stasi raus!" Stasi, get out!

As the streets filled with agitation, Warsaw Pact officials were looking fretfully at their countries' recent pasts. The Party line was that the Hungarian insurgency of 1956 had been provoked and promoted by Western-minded counter-revolutionaries. Now, in January 1989, Hungarian Politburo member Imre Pozsgay, chairman of a committee charged with studying the country's postwar history, reported to the Hungarian public in a radio interview that

"According to [our] research the committee judges what happened in 1956 to have been a popular uprising against an oligarchy that was humiliating the nation." He went on to say: "With this evaluation, the official standpoint approaches those of historians and public opinion. It is wrong," he emphasized, "to qualify the events as counter-revolution." Such a finding, however, was not yet "the official standpoint." Two weeks later, at a Central Committee meeting, Pozsgay was roasted by his colleagues. In the end, the Central Committee came up with a compromise: It endorsed the history committee's findings but resolved not to make the details public.

The Central Committee did make public its decision to exhume from an unmarked grave the remains of Imre Nagy, premier of the free Hungary briefly established by the 1956 revolution. Nagy would be reburied with due honors. On May 6, Radio Budapest rebroadcast the speech he had made at the beginning of the Soviet invasion. He had accused the Soviets of attempting "to overthrow the legal Hungarian democratic government." He was seized soon after he gave that speech and hidden away from family, friends, and colleagues; only two years later was he tried and executed. There is no obvious accounting for such quirks in Soviet justice. There had to have been a voice counseling that Nagy be kept alive. Why? Merely because he was a distinguished Hungarian official? But that was the principal reason, his accusers would have insisted, for executing him. Somewhere an archive on the subject exists. Somewhere, the scholar lives who will find it and write down what happened.

On June 16, six flag-draped coffins were brought into

Budapest's Heroes' Square. Five of them bore the bodies of Nagy and his chief lieutenants. The sixth coffin was empty. It represented the hundreds of Hungarians who were killed in the two weeks of fighting, or who were executed after the uprising was put down. The pallbearers included Imre Pozsgay and Hungary's new premier, Miklos Nemeth. The quarter of a million people in attendance included many émigrés who had returned for the occasion. At the interment that afternoon, the names were read out of 250 freedom fighters who had been subjected to show trials and then executed. The East German news service denounced the event, characterizing it as an "anti-Communist exercise engineered by the opposition."

August 21 was the twenty-first anniversary of the invasion of Czechoslovakia that turned the Prague Spring into a fresh winter. Three thousand demonstrators gathered in Wenceslaus Square. There would have been many more, but the regime had placed leading dissidents under house arrest and blocked roads leading to the square. The police endured twenty minutes of demonstrators singing the national anthem, shouting anti-Soviet slogans, and chanting the names of Dubcek and Havel. Then the police moved, swinging truncheons and arresting hundreds.

From surrounding countries, a variety of sentiments were recorded. The Polish Senate, by unanimous resolution, expressed "sorrow" over Poland's part in the 1968 invasion. The Hungarian government went on record as saying that it "did not concur with the 1968 intervention" but that any final judgment had to be made by the Czechoslovakians themselves. In East Germany, the old reliable *Neues Deutschland* explained that the invasion had been necessary to save Czechoslovakia from "imperialist forces." A spokesman for the Soviet Foreign Ministry said, "The events of 1968 in Czechoslovakia and around it must be seen in the political and international context of the time . . . The perception of the events and the reaction to them by the outside world was at the time in many respects derivative of the then level of confrontation between the two military-political blocs." Ambivalence had tied the tongue of the Soviet spokesman.

There had been rumors all that summer that Erich Honecker was dying. In July, he had fallen ill during a Warsaw Pact meeting in Bucharest and returned home early. But the trouble proved to be a gallstone—not cancer, as the rumors had it. And Honecker was in high good shape to preside over the German Democratic Republic's fortieth-anniversary celebration on October 6–7 in East Berlin. His guests of honor were Mikhail and Raisa Gorbachev. Milos Jakes, general secretary of the Czechoslovakian Communist Party, had come from Prague, and, from Warsaw, Wojciech Jaruzelski, still president of the reorganized Poland. Yao Yilin was there—vice premier of the Red Chinese regime that had just conducted the Tiananmen Square massacre. And Yasir Arafat, who was still running the PLO from Tunis while indigenous forces in Palestine were beginning the Intifada.

Honecker maneuvered to keep Gorbachev away from explicitly pro-democracy demonstrators. It would not do to have the supreme Communist in apparent spiritual union with the noisy dissidents in one of the satellite states. But

Gorbachev was cheered wherever he went. He and Honecker visited East Germany's Tomb of the Unknown Soldier, and the Soviet War Memorial, celebrating the Soviet soldiers killed in the Battle of Berlin, April–May 1945.

The two leaders went then to the Palace of the Republic to deliver major addresses. Gorbachev suggested, not for the first time, and using appropriate ellipses, that his host might want to try some of the liberalizations that had succeeded in the Soviet Union. But however intransigent he deemed the GDR, he took the same hands-off policy he had taken in dealing with reformist Budapest and Warsaw. "Policies that affect the German Democratic Republic," he said, "are decided not in Moscow but in Berlin." In his own speech, Honecker stated that he would never give in to the "revanchist," "neo-Nazi" West Germans and their allies, who had launched "an unbridled campaign of insults against the Communist German state."

That evening Gorbachev and Honecker stood side by side watching a torchlight parade of the FDJ (Free German Youth). The next day they were again side by side, this time to review a formal military parade. At the very time they were watching that parade, a special Party congress in Budapest was formally renouncing Marxism.

Honecker looked frail after his difficult summer, but managed throughout the festivities to appear resolute and triumphant, as if events had vindicated his policies.

After the military parade, Gorbachev talked with a group of journalists and spoke two oracular sentences: "I believe that dangers await only those who do not react to life. Anyone who seizes the impulses and realities of life, and forms his policies accordingly, should fear no difficulties."

. . .

Although Honecker was determined that demonstrations should not mar the anniversary celebration, they happened anyway—in Dresden, Potsdam, Leipzig, Magdeburg, and East Berlin itself. The marches following the candlelight vigils had been growing larger and larger. The climax, viewed retrospectively, came two days after the anniversary guests returned home, on October 9 in Leipzig. This would be the fourth Monday evening in the series, and it promised the biggest turnout yet. Honecker could stand it no longer. He ordered a massive crackdown. Some clue to what he had in mind is suggested by what he said to Yao Yilin during the celebrations: he publicly praised Red China's handling of the Tiananmen "counterrevolutionaries." But his own crackdown never materialized. Fifty thousand people marched safely in Leipzig, and triumphantly.

What exactly happened that evening was disputed. One account holds that Egon Krenz, a Politburo member and Honecker's longtime protégé, flew to Leipzig and personally countermanded Honecker's order. Another holds that Krenz did not actually go to Leipzig until several days later, and that the initiative to stay the hand of the security forces had come from Kurt Masur, director of the Gewandhaus Orchestra.

Whoever made the final decision, it is recorded that, on the weekend before the march, Masur invited two civilian public figures and three local officials of the Socialist Unity Party to meet at his home, where they drafted an appeal both to the demonstrators and to the Stasi and Volksarmee to avoid violence.

But someone had to give the order not to shoot, and it would not have been an orchestra conductor, however eminent. It may have been Krenz, who had the authority to do so as Politburo member for security. Or it may—this was Willy Brandt's speculation—have been the Soviet commander attached to the Volksarmee who intervened to protect the protesters.

On October 11, the East German Politburo held an emergency session. The protesters were formally denounced as "rampaging hooligans."

On the 13th, the GDR released the hundreds of protesters who had been arrested between October 3 and 9, and Honecker told a gathering in East Berlin that his regime was prepared to discuss matters with "all citizens."

On the 16th, more than a hundred thousand marched in Leipzig, and on the 18th, Honecker's retirement was announced. Krenz was named his successor as secretary-general of the Central Committee, chairman of the State Council, and chairman of the National Defense Council.

The following week was a busy one in the Eastern Bloc. On October 24, Soviet foreign minister Eduard Shevardnadze traveled to Warsaw for a regular meeting of the Warsaw Pact foreign ministers. Feeling his way, he told reporters that he hoped the Warsaw Pact would become more a political and less a military grouping. He suggested that both the Warsaw Pact and NATO be phased out.

October 28 would mark the seventy-first anniversary of

the founding of the Czechoslovak Republic in 1918. The groundwork for the Allies' establishment of the new state at the end of World War I had been laid by Tomas Masaryk, philosopher and Czechoslovakian patriot, who had traveled to Washington, D.C., and to Pittsburgh earlier that year to gain the support of President Wilson and of the principal organizations of Czech- and Slovak-Americans. It was his son, Jan, who died by defenestration thirty years later. Jan Masaryk was pushed out the window of his third-floor apartment at the Foreign Ministry building by Communist agents intending to discourage Czechoslovakian inclinations to resist Soviet domination.

In the days leading up to the anniversary, the authorities put a handful of human-rights activists under detention, including Vaclav Havel, who was nursing a bronchial infection. Times had indeed changed: Havel was taken to the hospital instead of to a jail cell or to the nearest window.

General Secretary Jakes and Premier Ladislav Adamec both reaffirmed their resistance to, as Jakes put it, "anti-socialist forces." Adamec, talking to reporters during a state visit to Austria, elaborated the point: "I am a supporter of the broadest democracy, but also of order and discipline and in no case of destabilization."

On the 28th, ten thousand people gathered in Wenceslaus Square. The anniversary celebration began peacefully, although the mood was not one of mere historical nostalgia: the crowd chanted "Freedom!" and "We want democracy," and there were banners calling for Jakes's ouster. The police indulged the demonstrators for an hour or two but then ordered them to evacuate the square. When they did not, policemen waded in, swinging their truncheons. Some 350 people were taken to prison. Many were injured, a dozen of them badly enough to require hospitalization.

That same week, Gorbachev paid a state visit to Helsinki. Among his entourage was Foreign Ministry spokesman Gerasimov, one of the freer spirits in the Soviet hierarchy. In Helsinki, Gerasimov explained to reporters how the Soviet Union's approach to its neighbors had changed. "The Brezhnev Doctrine is dead," he said. "You know the Frank Sinatra song 'My Way'? Hungary and Poland are doing it their way. We now have the Sinatra Doctrine."

Egon Krenz, at fifty-two, was the youngest member of the GDR Politburo, and ostentatiously so. Like his mentor, Honecker, he had made his career through the Free German Youth; unlike his more formal mentor, even after he was elevated to the Party's Central Committee he continued to dress like a young FDJ functionary. When he joined the Politburo in 1983, he was given the portfolio of youth affairs, but also a security portfolio. Now, in October 1989, that security portfolio was a serious hindrance to him in his efforts to convince the East German people that reform was at hand.

However, once Krenz succeeded Honecker, he quickly set to work in the spirit of Robespierre: *There go my followers—I must lead them.* On October 26, GDR officials opened formal talks with opposition leaders. On the 27th, an amnesty was announced for all who had been arrested for taking part in demonstrations—and for all who had left East Germany and might now want to return. On the

31st, Krenz traveled to Moscow to meet with Gorbachev. Upon leaving their private meeting Krenz told reporters that he was ready to put the Soviets' "vanguard experience" with perestroika and glasnost to work in East Germany. Asked about the unrest, he replied, "Many people are out on the streets to show that they want better socialism and a renovation of society. . . . I believe this is a good sign, an indication that we are at a turning point in the life of the German Democratic Republic."

On November 1, the Krenz regime reopened the border with Czechoslovakia. Thousands of East Germans poured across it. Krenz took to the airwaves to plead with those who had not yet left. "Trust our policy of renewal," he said. "Your place, dear fellow citizens, is here. We need you." But many of his fellow citizens were not disposed to trust him. We should trust him, a retired factory worker asked a *New York Times* reporter, "after he went to China to congratulate them for the blood they spilled?" Believe him, "after he rigged our last election? After being the boss of state security? The sparrows on the roof wouldn't believe him." A West German reporter quoted a comment about Krenz that had been making the rounds: "He can smile and laugh more readily than any of our leading comrades. But he can also smile and laugh as he orders a death sentence to be carried out."

Over the next few days, eleven of the GDR Politburo's eighteen members were retired, including two of the fathers of the Berlin Wall, Willi Stoph and Erich Mielke, who in the small hours of August 4, 1961, helped work out the details of the "secret seal-off matter."

The eleven retirees were replaced by four newcomers

to the regime. These included Hans Modrow, the Party chief of Dresden, who had been holding talks with local dissident leaders. On November 9, Gerasimov weighed in with the Soviet response to the personnel changes: "It's their country; they know better. But we welcome these changes."

During all this upheaval, Günter Schabowski, Politburo member and Party chief for East Berlin, was holding televised press conferences every evening. Foreign as well as local journalists were invited, and—yet another sign of change—the conferences were broadcast live in East Germany.

At about 9:00 P.M. on Thursday, November 9, the press conference seemed to be winding up when a reporter asked one final question. Hesitantly, and without looking into the camera, as if what he had to say was not entirely fit for public discussion, Schabowski pronounced magic words: *"Permanent emigration is henceforth allowed across all border crossing points between East Germany and West Germany and West Berlin."*

Viewers turned to each other in disbelief. . . . *Did he say what I thought he said?* Then, *Is this some kind of trick?*

A few decided to test out the words of manumission. There and then. A group of friends, who had been watching the televised press conference in a bar, quickly paid their bill and walked four blocks to the nearest border crossing, at Bornholmerstrasse. They showed their identity cards to the Grepo on duty. He permitted them to cross the bridge into West Berlin. One of them spoke to an

American reporter. "To walk across this bridge into West Berlin is the most normal thing in the world. But things haven't been normal here for twenty-eight years."

The news traveled with the speed of light. West Berliners also poured out into the streets. By midnight the whole area between the Brandenburg Gate and Checkpoint Charlie was one huge, joyous party. Car horns tooted, there was dancing in the streets, and champagne, or a reasonable substitute, was raised in toasts, drunk, and sprayed around the assembly.

There were tears too, of relief, of sadness for wasted years, of mourning for those who had died trying to escape. One young man said in wonderment, "I couldn't imagine that I'd ever just be able to walk through the Brandenburg Gate. It's unreal, unbelievable." Willy Brandt told a group of revelers, "Nothing will be the same again."

The Grepos found themselves in a disciplinary quandary for which nothing in their training had prepared them. Some made a great fussy show of examining people's papers. Some responded spontaneously, even if dazed, to hands extended in greeting. One young Grepo found himself in an undreamed-of position: a microphone was thrust at him, and intense light aimed in his face. The television reporter's question was, "What do you think of the whole thing?" He replied judiciously, with words heard round the world: "The last twelve hours, travel possibilities have improved enormously."

The idea hit a vigorous young man: Why not climb up onto the wall itself? The hundred yards stretching out on either side of the Brandenburg Gate were well situated. This was the section that had a wide, flat top, not the big cylindrical pipes that the Honecker regime had used to replace the barbed wire on the rest of the wall. Many followed suit. Even the tallest wall-climbers needed a leg up, and the less athletic were also given a hand from above. Press accounts spoke of celebrants dancing on the wall, but this could not go on for very long. There was no room. The exultant Berliners satisfied themselves, linking arms left and right, merely to sway their hips.

At dawn on Friday the party began to break up. The Eastern celebrants mostly drifted back to their homes. If East Berlin wasn't a prison any more, why *not* go home?

Already on Thursday evening someone had improvised a chisel, and the first piece of the wall was broken off. On Friday, hundreds of Berliners, West and East, were there with real chisels and claw hammers and screwdrivers and sledgehammers to pry loose their own piece of the wall. Resident foreigners joined in. Some shared their souvenirs with people back home whom they deemed persistent friends of a free Berlin. (Reporter Bennett Owen kindly sent one to *National Review*'s managing editor.) On Saturday, official East German workers arrived on the scene. Some used jackhammers to widen openings in the wall; others set about restoring the streets and resetting the rail lines that had been ripped up twenty-eight years before. On Sunday, the wall came down at Potsdamerplatz, and West Berlin's mayor, Walter Momper, declared, "The heart of Berlin will soon beat again."

Chancellor Kohl was in Warsaw when he got the news. He cut short his visit to fly to Berlin. He stood on the steps of City Hall, where John Kennedy had addressed Berliners twenty-six years before. "I want to call out to all in the German Democratic Republic," Kohl said. "We're on your side. We are, and remain, one nation. We belong together. Long live a free German fatherland. Long live a united Europe."

His government offered 100 Marks (about $55) in "greeting money" to any Easterner who wanted to come over and see the western half of Berlin. Thousands did so, flocking wide-eyed to the shops on the Kurfürstendamm, shops they had seen on TV in their "nightly emigration." They couldn't buy much with 100 Marks. But they could express delight and awe at such a profusion of goods. They had in years past expressed proper pride in the relative strength of their own economy, up against those of the other satellites. But it was nothing like what they now saw, even if they could not taste it.

In my column written on November 10, I began: "When the news came in, President Bush sat quietly in his large chair in the Oval Office and said in grave tones that we must not overreact. He is absolutely right about this. *Jingle bells! Jingle bells! Jingle all the wayyyy!* It is proper to deem it a historical development, but its significance must not affect our judgment. *Oh, what a beautiful mor-ning! Oh, what a beau-ti-ful day!!!* After all, there is tomorrow to think about in Germany *Germany?!?! What do you mean, 'Germany'? You mean West Germany or you mean East Germany?* and the score allows for many variations. Calmness is in order."

The holiday atmosphere at the wall continued for days. Many, including Grepos and Vopos, stood in the new openings posing for photographs. A popular slogan in the pro-democracy movement, "Die Mauer muss weg"—"The wall must go"—had been among the graffiti on the western side of the wall. Now someone wrote on the *eastern* side: "Die Mauer IST Weg."

The breaching of the wall sent waves of euphoria through the Free World. But many were afraid to hope that this was truly a turning point, not a culminating point. Eastern European émigrés in particular expressed doubt that their own native countries would experience similar relief. "Oh, it's wonderful, wonderful," a Czech waiter in New York told a customer a few days after November 9, "but nothing like that could happen in Czechoslovakia. My people are too demoralized. They'll never rebel." At the time, he seemed to be right. Ever since the brutal suppression of the October 28 demonstration, the streets of Prague had been quiet.

Then on Friday, November 17, the Czechoslovak Youth Union held a rally, with government permission, in honor of two students who had been killed fifty years before while protesting the Nazi takeover. The rally turned into a pro-democracy demonstration and was decisively put down by the police. It was reported that one protester, a mathematics student named Martin Smid, had been beaten to death. The government first denied responsibility, then said the charge itself was phony. Not one but two youths claiming to be "Martin Smid" were shown alive and well on state television.

Whatever actually happened to Smid, every day the following week there were strikes and protests. On Monday, the 20th, two hundred thousand demonstrators marched peacefully in Prague. For the first time since 1968 there were also demonstrations in other Czechoslovakian cities. The following day, Premier Adamec began talks with the principal opposition group, Civic Forum, modeled on the East German New Forum. After that meeting, Vaclav Havel, standing on a balcony in Wenceslaus Square, reported to a crowd of one hundred fifty thousand that Adamec had promised not to impose martial law and had said he would be willing to bring non-Communists into the government. A Czech priest, Father Vaclav Maly, also spoke to the crowd. He read an incendiary letter from Frantisek Cardinal Tomasek, the primate of Czechoslovakia. "We are surrounded by countries that have broken the bars of totalitarianism. We cannot wait any more. We need democratic government."

On Thursday, the 23rd, Alexander Dubcek addressed a crowd of seventy thousand in Bratislava. This was his first public appearance since his ouster in 1969. On Friday he came to Prague—again, for the first time since 1969—and addressed two hundred thousand people in Wenceslaus Square. "Long live socialism with a human face," he said. "Long live our new generation." Also on Friday, General Secretary Jakes led the Presidium in a mass resignation. However, six of his colleagues were reappointed to the Presidium by the Central Committee. On Saturday, Havel told some eight hundred thousand of his fellow citizens that the shakeup was a "trick."

Two weeks earlier, Gorbachev had responded to the opening of the wall by admonishing the West against opportunizing on the changes in Eastern Europe. Now he published an article in *Pravda* defining his own perestroika as an attempt to give socialism a "human face." This wording was widely viewed as an homage to Dubcek.

On December 10, a coalition government with more non-Communist than Communist members was sworn in, and Wenceslaus Square was filled once more, this time not in anger but in joy. Dubcek and Havel both declared their candidacy for president, but the following week Dubcek withdrew in Havel's favor. On December 28, the Federal Assembly elected Dubcek as its Speaker, and the day after that elected Havel president. He was the first non-Communist president of Czechoslovakia since Eduard Benes, forty-one years before. The Velvet Revolution was gathering speed.

Todor Zhivkov of Bulgaria was the senior surviving secretary-general in the Eastern Bloc. He had begun his iron rule in 1954, just one year after the death of Stalin. Now the shock waves reached even his country. On November 3 there was a demonstration in Sofia. It was sponsored by an illegal environmental group, Eco-Glasnost, and nine thousand people took part.

That figure was pathetic by standards recently set in Poland, Hungary, East Germany, and Czechoslovakia. In

Zhivkov's redoubt it was earth-shaking. On November 10, Zhivkov stunned his Central Committee colleagues by resigning from both the Party leadership and the presidency. His hastily chosen successor, Foreign Minister Petar Mladenov, announced quickly that there was "no alternative to restructuring." He cautioned, though, that changes would take place "only within the framework of socialism, in the name of socialism, and on the road to socialism." But by the end of the year, seven weeks later, the Central Committee had renounced the Party's monopoly on power, and Mladenov had scheduled talks with the newborn Union of Democratic Forces.

That left one holdout, apart from the Soviet Union itself: Romania. A Romanian-born bicycle repairman in San Diego echoed the disbelief of the Czech waiter in New York: "I'm so happy for the Germans and the Czechs. But of course nothing like that could happen in Romania, not till Ceausescu dies. He has too tight a hold—the people are too afraid of him."

Until the mid-Sixties, Romania had been, so to speak, an ordinary, well-behaved Soviet satellite. Under Gheorghe Gheorghiu-Dej, Romania was totalitarian, but a state in which there was some room to maneuver. When Gheorghiu-Dej died and Nicolae Ceausescu took over, he set about closing up that room. He strengthened and molded the Securitate, the secret police. They were now the equivalent of the Gestapo, the Stasi, the KGB. He instituted his "systemization" program. Rural villages were destroyed, peasant families forcibly relocated. This anti-kulak–style program was to lead to grand new agricultural collectives, which, however, never materialized. Agricultural production dropped catastrophically. Much of what was produced was sold abroad to acquire the funds necessary to maintain the Securitate.

Ceausescu also generated a massive personality cult. His picture was everywhere, printed on posters, woven into tapestries, painted on walls. In Bucharest nine thousand houses and sixteen historic churches were bulldozed in order to create the Boulevard of Socialist Victory—an eight-lane road sweeping up to the Palace of Parliament. Before World War II and the Communist takeover, Bucharest had been the most elegant city in the region. Now, British journalist Anthony Daniels remarked that Ceausescu seemed determined to turn the Paris of the Balkans into the Pyongyang of the Balkans.

Ceausescu was not prepared to go quietly, like Zhivkov. When opposition started to emerge, Ceausescu moved quickly to cut it down. In March 1989, a group of retired Party and government officials published an open letter accusing him of human-rights violations and demanding an end to the systemization program. All six signatories were arrested. Efforts to communicate with them were blocked.

Then, in December, protests broke out in Timisoara, a city in the Transylvanian region, near Romania's borders with Hungary and Yugoslavia. The protests were sparked by government harassment of the Reverend Laszlo Tokes, a Protestant minister who had been set upon and stabbed by a band of masked men, almost certainly members of the Securitate. On December 16 the protests evolved into a full-scale demonstration. Ceausescu reacted as Honecker had intended to react to the marchers in Leipzig. Army and

Securitate forces, including tank and helicopter units, moved in and started firing. The death toll was estimated at an extraordinary four thousand. The United States, Britain, Poland, and even the Soviet Union issued protests. Ceausescu was not in Bucharest to receive them. He was in Iran, going ahead with a scheduled state visit.

On December 20, Ceausescu returned to Bucharest and blasted the "fascists" and "terrorists" who were stirring up dissent. The next day at noon he stood on the balcony of the Palace of Parliament to address his people. Television cameras captured the astonishment on his face when his people began to boo and jeer him. Securitate forces swung into action to disperse the crowd. The first casualties were two young men crushed beneath an armored car. Fighting continued through the night, with an estimated forty dead in Bucharest and another thirty in Cluj, a small city in Transylvania. But as protests erupted in other parts of the country, reports came in that army units were refusing to help the Securitate suppress them.

On the morning of December 22, Radio Bucharest announced that Defense Minister Vasile Milea had committed suicide. Neither foreign diplomats in Bucharest nor the Romanian General Staff believed it: they suspected that Milea had been killed by Securitate officers in retaliation for the army's failure to support them.

That may have been the decisive event. When one hundred fifty thousand protesters gathered later that day in Bucharest's University Square, the army actively joined them in beating back the Securitate. The insurgents captured the Palace of Parliament, the Central Committee headquarters, and other government buildings. That evening the liberated Radio Bucharest announced the formation of the National Salvation Front, which would include Laszlo Tokes and General Stefan Gusa, chief of the General Staff.

Soon after the announcement, Nicolae and Elena Ceausescu, who had fled Bucharest by helicopter that morning, were captured by armed insurgents and handed over to the military. On Christmas Day they were put on trial by a self-described "extraordinary military tribunal" and charged with committing genocide, abusing power, undermining the economy, and stealing government funds. For fear that the Securitate would come in with a last-minute rescue, the army did not disclose the site of the trial, and no outside observers were permitted. However, the proceedings were videotaped, and the entire trial was broadcast on Romanian television the following day. The day after that, we in America could see a short clip on our own television screens—an elderly couple huddled in their overcoats and looking bewildered and almost pitiable. Almost. One of Nicolae Ceausescu's replies to his interrogators reflected his posture. "I am the president of Romania and the commander in chief of the Romanian army. I am the president of the people. I will not speak with you provocateurs any more, and I will not speak with the organizers of the putsch."

As for Elena Ceausescu, she was no innocent bystander. She was a Politburo member and first deputy premier. A few months earlier, when it appeared that ill health might force her husband to step down, she started jockeying for position to succeed him. Now, at the trial, she occasionally piped up with remarks like "Such impudence! I am a member and the chairwoman of the Academy of Sciences. You cannot talk to me in such a way!"

The trial was not a model of due process (although the Ceausescus were offered a defense counsel, whose services they indignantly refused). But there is no doubt that the couple had done the things they were accused of.

They were sentenced to death by firing squad. Then there ensued macabre confusion. Accounts differ. Perhaps the officer in charge of the firing squad was apprehensive that the Securitate forces, still active, would storm in before the executioners could do their job. Perhaps he and the squad members were awestruck at having in their power the dictators who had oppressed them for so long. Whatever. The result was disorder. The soldiers didn't wait for the formal order to fire, starting to pull their triggers as soon as the Ceausescus stepped outside the building. No one knows how many bullets were fired, but photographs showed the bloody remains.

Warehouses broken open by the insurgents after the execution confirmed the widespread belief that, while most Romanians lived in destitution, Party leaders were copiously supplied with luxuries, including beef, chocolate, coffee, and oranges. As Elena Ceausescu was being led to the firing squad, she cried out, "I was like a mother to you!" Mother ate off gold dishes, the kids starved.

Soon after taking power, Nicolae Ceausescu had outlawed Christmas. Now, against the grisly background of his and Elena's execution, with the fighting still continuing, Romanians celebrated the Feast of the Nativity for the first time in more than twenty years.

.   .   .

As East Germany was spinning toward the future, Egon Krenz struggled desperately to keep his balance. The opening of the borders relieved some of the pressure, but the pro-democracy forces still wanted—democracy. On the evening of Monday, November 13, two hundred thousand marched in Leipzig. Reisenfreiheit, freedom to travel, having been achieved, they now demanded free elections, and just plain freedom.

Trying to shore up his position, Krenz had scheduled an extraordinary congress of the Socialist Unity Party for the following May. He now moved the extraordinary congress forward to December. On November 22, the Politburo announced that it was willing to enter into roundtable talks with "other political forces" in the country. On December 1, the Volkskammer nullified the clause in the East German constitution that mandated for the Socialist Unity Party the "leading role" in the government. But the protesters were not to be appeased by half measures. A poll showed Krenz as having the support of only 9.6 percent of the people. Hans Modrow, the new premier, who as Party chief of Dresden had held conciliatory talks with the dissidents, came in with 42 percent.

The final blow came with the publication of a series of articles in *Neues Deutschland*. The official Party newspaper had suddenly developed an interest in investigative reporting. The discrepancies the paper disclosed between the lifestyles of the rulers and the ruled in the Workers' and Peasants' State were not so large as in Romania, but they stirred great and righteous anger. Apart from descriptions of the luxurious houses in the Wandlitz compound, there were auxiliary revelations. Harry Tisch, head of the Free

German Trade Union Federation, kept a huge estate on the Baltic coast with a full complement of servants. Secretary of State for Foreign Trade Alexander Schalck-Golodkowski had been using public money to make private deals in the international arms market. Honecker and his colleagues collectively had billions of dollars in Swiss bank accounts.

On December 2, an investigating committee appointed by the Volkskammer brought in its report: the newspaper's allegations were all too true. At an emergency meeting the next day, the Central Committee expelled 12 of the Party's leading members, including Honecker, Stoph, Mielke, Tisch, and Schalck-Golodkowski. Upon which the entire Politburo (including Krenz and Modrow) resigned, followed by all 163 members of the Central Committee. But the machinery of government continued to operate. Tisch was arrested and imprisoned. Honecker was placed under house arrest at Wandlitz. Schalck-Golodkowski fled the country but soon gave himself up. He had used the same escape route others had used for twenty-eight years, but he did not need to climb over the wall, en route to West Berlin.

On December 6, Krenz resigned his government posts, and on December 8 the promised Extraordinary Party Congress convened in a sports complex in East Berlin. In a marathon session lasting seventeen hours, the delegates chose as their new Party leader the young Gregor Gysi, a lawyer who had represented New Forum clients. Before the balloting began, Gysi told the Congress, "We have to make a radical break with the Stalinist past. We have to change our ways of thinking."

On December 16, the Congress reconvened to take care of housekeeping details. Two communications were read out loud. Mikhail Gorbachev, in a telegram, expressed his support for the changes in East Germany. Erich Honecker, in a letter, took "full responsibility" for the crisis in his country. He had simply been "out of touch with real life" in East Germany, he said, though he added that he had been misled by others.

The Party decided to change its name. It had been the Socialist Unity Party of Germany (SED). Now it would be the Socialist Unity Party of Germany–Party of Democratic Socialism (SED–PDS). By such a measure, Herr Gysi explained with a straight face, both the traditionalists and the reformers would be accommodated. The momentous news was immediately ahead: the delegates were informed that the Stasi would be disbanded. Legitimate intelligence functions would be transferred to a civilian agency.

On December 19, Kohl traveled to Dresden to meet with Modrow, who had retained his post as premier. They came to agreement on some economic questions and on ending remaining travel restrictions between the two Germanies. On one matter, however, as Modrow put it, "the chancellor has his vision of the future, I have mine." Kohl's vision was of a united Germany. He spoke about this to a crowd of more than ten thousand in front of Dresden's Frauenkirche. The church had been destroyed by bombing during World War II, but, like the remains of old Coventry Cathedral, the remains of the Frauenkirche had been left standing in the postwar reconstruction. "When the historic moment makes it possible," Kohl told the crowd, he would work "for the unity of our nation."

He wished the Dresdeners a merry Christmas, and added, "God bless our German fatherland."

On New Year's Eve, Berliners gathered at the border as they had on the night of November 9. This time the festivities were organized, and included a mammoth fireworks show. There were tears and laughter, and they seemed no less genuine than at the spontaneous celebration seven weeks earlier. Whatever the 1990s would bring, the hated and dreaded wall, grim, endless reminder of the reach of totalitarian rule, was effectively gone. What was left of it was now a symbol of regeneration and hope.

5

The End of the Cold War

The changes in Eastern Europe were spectacular, exhilarating. But how easily could Eastern Europeans breathe, how securely plan, with the great superpower next door? Granted that Mikhail Gorbachev had proved amenable to Ronald Reagan and Margaret Thatcher. Still, he had the world's most massive army and a nuclear inventory second to none. *National Review*'s cover for the first issue of 1989 had shown Lenin through a shattered pane of glass. The caption: "The Coming Crack-Up of Communism." The accompanying story was by Radek Sikorski, who argued persuasively that the Soviet Union was a dying organism, crushed by the weight of its tyranny. Sikorski knew the Communist world from the inside, from his native Poland, which he would one day serve as deputy minister of defense. Yet despite it all—the breakup of the Warsaw Pact, the defeat in Afghanistan, and the internal dynamics Gorbachev had unleashed with his glasnost and perestroika—the basic Soviet structure stood. It was possible that the Soviet power would last through to the end of the century. And possible that it would end in a

Götterdämmerung that would care not at all about such niceties as tearing down the Berlin Wall.

Meanwhile, each of the old Soviet satellites was trying to figure out where it was heading. "Getting rid of Communism is proving not like casting off chains and suddenly walking free again," Sikorski wrote. Rather it was "like dropping some weight out of a heavy rucksack on a long slog toward elusive highlands." These nation-states all, even Bulgaria, sometime within the memory of their senior citizens had had some experience of civil society and rule of law, but for most, it had been brief. Only Czechoslovakia had had, between the twentieth century's two world wars, a modern representative democracy and a Western-style free-market economy. These countries had all been battered by the world wars, and now they were just emerged from two generations of political despotism and centrally planned economic disaster, compounded by the Kremlin's forcing them to tailor their production not to their own needs but to the Soviet Union's.

On the political front, there were odd denominational problems. How exactly to define an ex-Communist? How to judge the man who had renounced Communism? Which of the self-described ex-Communists were just dressing up in new party names, like the Democratic Left Alliance in Poland or the Socialist Party in Hungary? On the economic front, how to privatize the socialist concentrates left from the regimes just now forsworn?

Professor Milton Friedman, Nobel laureate and dean of free-market learning, published his warning in *National Review.* "The transition to freedom cannot be accomplished overnight," he wrote. "The formerly totalitarian societies have developed institutions, public attitudes, and vested interests that are wholly antithetical to the rapid creation of the basic economic requisites for freedom and prosperity," the most important of these being the secure ownership of private property and a stable monetary system. Not only, he warned, would reform-minded former satellites face internal obstacles. They would also be receiving advice and exhortation from the advanced Western nations. "Countries seeking to imitate the success of the West will make a great mistake if they pattern their policies on the current situation in the West rather than on what the situation was when the Western countries were at the stage the Eastern European countries are at now. Only our attained wealth enables us to support such wasteful, overblown government sectors. Hong Kong is a far better model for them than the U.S., Great Britain, or Sweden."

In East Germany itself, the transition began slowly. The New Forum was only a few weeks old when it effected the fall of the wall. There hadn't been such time as Poland's Solidarity had had to meditate on what it would do if the oppressive regime crumbled. By December 1989, East Germany's old guard (the *Alt-Herren Riege,* as they were known—the squad of old gentlemen) had fled or been removed from power. But they were replaced not by dissidents but by a younger generation of Communists. These men, led by Gregor Gysi and Hans Modrow, were political reformers, but not ideological reformers. They were, much like Gorbachev, bent on reforming the system in order to preserve it. They were not like Hungary's Imre

Pozsgay, who indeed wanted structural change and economic freedom.

The East German people were at first prepared to wait and see, wait and see if the new rulers would carry out the promises made by the Extraordinary Party Congress—especially the promises to hold elections in May 1990 and to begin immediately transferring the Stasi's legitimate functions to civilian control. As an earnest of substantive reforms to come, the regime changed the Stasi's formal name from Ministry of State Security to Office of National Security. But whatever the reduced functions of the new security agency, on January 8 the official in charge of the disbanding operation admitted that sixty thousand of the hundred thousand full-time Stasi officers were still on the payroll. It was widely speculated that even if the Office of National Security were nominally disbanded, it would bureaucratically reconstitute itself, with another new name but substantially the same personnel.

On January 15 the New Forum called for a pro-democracy rally outside Stasi headquarters in East Berlin. One hundred thousand turned up. The rally began peaceably but then exploded into emblematic violence: a rampage through the Stasi building. Several thousand demonstrators broke through the line of police guarding the building and pushed inside. They tore about gloriously through the filing cabinets, destroying some files and throwing others out the windows. Plenty would remain, but this was the physical enactment of the chants during the protest marches before the wall came down: "Stasi raus!" Stasi . . . get-up-and-get-out.

. . .

East Germany had always been a special case. Except for Bulgaria and Romania, it was the most rigidly centralized politically, and collectivized economically, of the satellite states. It needed to purge not only its Communist past, but also the dozen years of Nazi rule. But it had the advantage of an industrial base and a work ethos, so that it had developed the most successful economy of any of the Warsaw Pact states, including the Soviet Union. And, uniquely, in West Germany it had a Western counterpart.

These facts shaped the way Germans on both sides of the border reacted to their turning point. Starting, roughly, with the twenty-fifth anniversary of the Berlin Wall, European and American academics and journalists had been explaining why, no matter what happened in the evolution of Communism in Eastern Europe, Germany could never reunite. The two Germanies, they said, were now separate countries, with different cultures and ways of life. "Reunification" was a vision only of elderly romantics, remembering the Germany of their childhood—or of Nazi revanchists dreaming of a Fourth Reich. These observers cited polls taken in East Germany showing that, starting in the Seventies, a majority no longer considered reunification the number-one priority. The 70 to 80 percent of West Germans who consistently told pollsters they supported reunification were dismissed as merely paying lip service to the idea. Even so acute an observer as Peter Wyden—in his big book *Wall: The Inside Story of Divided Berlin,* published just a few months before the wall came down—wrote that "reunification is a dead herring issue . . . Regardless of their wishes, most Germans themselves are convinced that the prospect of a single Germany is a fantasy."

The events cascaded in. In March 1990, East Germany held its first free election since 1932. In that election, the center-right coalition of parties corresponding to West Germany's Christian Democrats and Free Democrats won a stunning victory—53 percent of the vote. The East German branch of the Social Democratic Party took 22 percent. The Communists, now known simply as the Party of Democratic Socialism, got a mere 16 percent. And the center-right had explicitly campaigned on the issue of reunification, with Chancellor Kohl taking an active part in the campaign.

Once the reunification train had been set in motion, it rolled down the tracks relentlessly. There were obstacles at many levels. France and Britain were cautious, the Tokyo bond market was jittery, East Germans were apprehensive about the Soviet response to the stationing of NATO troops on Eastern soil, West Germans were nervous about the huge cost of absorbing the pollution-ridden Eastern infrastructure. But nothing stood up against the passion, once ignited, to end the forty-five-year-long separation.

At midnight on October 2, 1990, the German Democratic Republic ceased to exist. In a televised speech, Chancellor Kohl thanked the Four Powers for signing the papers ending the occupation of Germany. At the official ceremony in Berlin, President Richard von Weizsäcker spoke of the nation's "thankfulness and joy" but also of its "burden of history." A million people celebrated in Berlin as the Federal Republic's black, red, and gold flag was raised in front of the Reichstag.

Not everyone rejoiced. The next day eight thousand opponents of reunification protested in Berlin, smashing windows, setting cars on fire, and fighting with riot police. In Leipzig, the Reverend Christian Führer—the pastor of St. Nicholas Church, where the candlelight marches had originated—explained why he was not ringing the church bells in celebration. There were, he said, too many scars remaining. So, "we will simply keep quiet and let the silence move people to think."

The projected costs of reunification were staggering: $34 billion just to bring East Germany's telephone system up to the standards of West Germany's, $63 billion for roads and railroads, $16 billion for unemployment benefits, $18 billion to cope with East German government debt, and on and on. Intimidating sums, up against the cost of Freikauf; huge even compared to the cost of the subsidies West Germany had been paying just to keep West Berlin afloat. But more than 70 percent of West Germans had said they were willing to pay whatever reunification cost.

As for the wall itself, much of it had been torn down by the time I returned to Berlin, in June 1990, to film a *Firing Line* special at the Reichstag. Three stretches of the wall were deliberately left standing, graffiti and all, as a "memorial for international freedom"—notably one a mile long in the eastern district of Friedrichshain, called the East Side Gallery. Nearby, south of the Spree River, one watchtower also was left standing. Its ground floor houses the Museum of Forbidden Art, displaying works by artists who had been outlawed by the East German regime. The upper floor has been preserved exactly as it was on November 9, 1989.

. . .

A major question, pondered before and after reunification, was: What would be condign punishment for those who had imposed so much suffering? There was no way to make restitution to the men and women who had been shot at the border, or held in prison for one political crime or another, or kept in the East for decades while separated spouse or children, unreachable, lived in the West. But something was owing to these victims of Communism. Ulbricht had not lived to see the destruction of his life's endeavor, and Honecker had escaped house arrest at Wandlitz and fled to Moscow. But there were plenty of remaining targets.

In the weeks after November 9, Stasi offices were stormed in various cities around East Germany. Stasi commissars in three of those cities committed suicide. But not one was lynched or executed. When high officials were arrested, there was heated debate over exactly what to charge them with. Erich Mielke was initially accused of corruption and of "damaging the national economy." In January 1990, prosecutors added charges of conspiring to order illegal surveillance of citizens and of violating the constitution—the paper instrument of 1949 suddenly reified, all those illusory rights staring into the face of the defendants. Thus Mielke was also charged with ordering violent attacks on peaceful demonstrations. A warrant was issued for Honecker's arrest on charges of manslaughter, citing his shoot-to-kill order, but the Soviets refused to turn him over. Egon Krenz was charged with manslaughter; Markus Wolf, as head of the foreign-espionage branch of the Stasi, with treason.

As for lower-ranking Stasi and Grepos, most Germans were inclined to accept the excuse, notwithstanding that it had been so widely derided when used by low-level Nazis, "I was just following orders." One former Grepo (who had escaped from East Berlin in the Sixties by leaping from a height of nine yards, badly injuring both feet) made a novel, and plausible, point to historian Anthony Kemp: Yes, he said, over the course of Germany's division hundreds of people were deliberately killed while trying to escape, and many more were captured and imprisoned. But given how many succeeded in escaping, do you really think most Grepos were *trying* to follow orders?

The Germans ended up deciding that the way to establish rule of law in the new polity was on no account to engage in what would be seen as victor's justice. Some of the early criminal convictions, for activity not considered criminal when done, were set aside by higher courts. Thus various charges initially made against Mielke were withdrawn. Instead, he was convicted, piquantly, of the assassination of two Berlin police officers—in 1931, when, as a Communist, he was agitating against the Weimar Republic. Krenz had been convicted of manslaughter, and the conviction stood, but he served only six years in prison. Wolf's pleading that he had been not a treasonous citizen of the Federal Republic, but rather a loyal citizen of the Democratic Republic, was accepted fatalistically. He was convicted on the lesser charge of ordering kidnappings from across the East–West border, which was illegal under East as well as West German law, and given a two-year sentence, suspended. Lower-ranking Stasi officers were charged not with manslaughter but with embezzlement. None of these officials or officers was executed. Some spent months in prison, others a few years.

But clemency for individuals didn't go on to absolution for what they had done. Surviving Stasi files were carefully scrutinized. The focus achieved gave a true idea of the unmatched thoroughness of the East German police state. Simon Wiesenthal, no less, expert on the crimes of the Nazis, told the American researcher John Koehler, "The Stasi was much, much worse than the Gestapo, if you consider only the oppression of its own people." There are many ways to give an idea of the intensity of the oppression. Bare numbers tell their own story. Koehler writes, "To ensure that the people would become and remain submissive, East German communist leaders saturated their realm with more spies than had any other totalitarian government in recent history." The KGB had about 1 agent per 5,830 citizens. The Nazis, according to Wiesenthal's figures, had 1 Gestapo officer per 2,000 citizens. The Stasi had 1 officer per 166 citizens.

It wasn't merely the officers that the GDR depended on. The Stasi had a whole stable of regular informers, the inoffizielle Mitarbeiter (unofficial collaborators). The IMs outnumbered the full-time officers nearly two to one. Add the more casual stool pigeons and, as Koehler puts it, "it would not have been unreasonable to assume that at least one Stasi informer was present in any party of ten or twelve dinner guests."

The End

Mikhail Gorbachev survived in power through 1990, but his empire was crumbling and he was losing interest in its outer reaches. Markus Wolf quotes in his memoirs from a reproachful letter he addressed to Gorbachev in October of that year: "We were your friends. We wear a lot of your country's decorations on our breasts. We were said to have made a great contribution to your security. Now, in our hour of need, I assume that you will not deny us your help." What Wolf wanted from Gorbachev was straightforward: to make his signing the end-of-occupation papers dependent on an amnesty for East German spies. Gorbachev didn't even raise the question in his talks with Chancellor Kohl. "It was the Soviets' ultimate betrayal of their East German friends, whose work for over four decades had strengthened Soviet influence in Europe," Wolf wrote.

The year 1991 began with Soviet troops attacking protesters in Lithuania. Fifteen civilians were killed. That deed led to the usual criticisms from around the world, but also to one unusual criticism. Comrade Boris Yeltsin, president of the Russian Federation, called on Russian soldiers to disobey any such order in the future. He then mutinously pondered establishing a Russian "defense force," to protect the republic from the Kremlin.

This led to an intensification of the battle between Gorbachev and Yeltsin, which included calls for each other's resignation. Gorbachev also took a turn on the international stage by requesting to be invited to the Group of Seven meeting in London that July. "I am already thinking over what I will say," he told a news conference in Moscow. "And if I am not there, I will say it anyway." After appeals by French president François Mitterrand and Chancellor Kohl, President Bush agreed that Gorbachev should be invited to the meeting as an observer. Gorbachev duly attended, and he succeeded in getting various forms of technical assistance; but he did not get the direct aid he was really after. Before returning home, he arranged for Kohl and the new British prime minister, John Major, to visit him in Moscow later in the year. He did not foresee the problems, later in the year, of receiving official visitors.

On August 5, Gorbachev left for his usual summer vacation at his dacha in the Crimea. He planned to return to Moscow on August 20 to sign a freshly negotiated "union treaty," devolving certain powers in the Union of Soviet Socialist Republics from the Kremlin to the constituent republics. At 6:00 A.M. on Monday, August 19, TASS, the official Soviet news agency, announced that Gorbachev was incapacitated by illness and that something called the "State Committee for the State of Emergency" was exercising power in his place.

For the world abroad, this turning point was different from the Hungarian Revolution, the building of the Berlin Wall, or the crushing of the Prague Spring. Different even from the recent opening of the Berlin Wall. This was a very great moment that we in the West could watch live, minute by minute, on CNN. The images we saw were great wrenches from Marxist history and Soviet nationalism. There were the Soviet tanks rumbling through the streets of Moscow on missions unknown, and civilians pulling up paving stones to use as weapons. At 11:00 A.M. on Monday, just five hours after the TASS announcement, a burly white-haired man in a business suit appeared on screen. He was standing on a Soviet tank and addressing the crowd around him. Boris Yeltsin had acted heroically, and within two days the hard-liners' coup had been frustrated.

At the end of eleven delirious days in August, the Supreme Soviet voted to suspend all activity done in the name of the Communist Party. In December, the Union of Soviet Socialist Republics was officially redesignated. It was now the Commonwealth of Independent States. The great Communist monolith that had dominated international life was dead, a wreck from within.

Reactions were national, corporate, public, individual. I record my own summary, given at a celebration of *National Review* magazine, founded in substantial measure to urge on the struggle against the Soviet Union. "I was nineteen years old at the time the Yalta conference was held. Soon after that came Potsdam, and the West lost Eastern Europe to the Communists. The Cold War had begun. On the last day of August, one month ago, the Communist Party was banned in the Soviet Union. Coincidentally, I am sixty-five years old. I passed from teenage to senior citizenship, coinciding with the duration of the Cold War.

"We can sleep better for knowing that our cousins have regained their freedom. But we can't bring back those who lost their lives, nor bring back lifetimes in freedom to those who spent theirs without it."

Might millions of those people have been spared the

heavy hand of Soviet repression if the Allies, led by the United States, had taken direct counteraction at various turning points in the Cold War? Say, in 1948, when the Soviets applied their salami tactics to the countries of Eastern Europe? Or in 1953, during the East Berlin riots? Or in 1956, 1961, 1968? When change finally did come in those countries, it came most directly from resistance done by their own people—to be sure, with moral support from the West, plus some direct initiatives from sympathetic leaders, notably Ronald Reagan, Margaret Thatcher, and Pope John Paul II.

But the rise and fall of the Berlin Wall were great moments. It stood more than twice as many years as Hitler ruled Germany, yet finally it yielded, to a human spirit that took a half century but, finally, effected the liberation of the whole of that part of Germany that made its way from the Democratic Republic of Germany, to the democratic republic of Germany.

Notes

1: Ulbricht's Berlin Problem

pp. 5–8: *Facts on File* (hereafter *FoF*) (New York: Facts on File) 1958, pp. 361–362, 373, 389–390; Lucius D. Clay, *Decision in Germany* (Garden City, N.Y.: Doubleday, 1950), pp. 15–30; Peter Wyden, *Wall: The Inside Story of Divided Berlin* (New York: Simon and Schuster, 1989), pp. 55, 72; Curtis Cate, *The Ides of August: The Berlin Wall Crisis—1961* (New York: M. Evans, 1978), pp. 25–26.

pp. 8–13: Giles MacDonogh, *Berlin: A Portrait of Its History, Politics, Architecture, and Society* (New York: St. Martin's Press, 1997), pp. 6–7, 45, 76, 108–110, 344–347, 440–443; *Green Guide, Germany* (Watford, Eng.: Michelin, 1998), pp. 81–88; *Berlin* (London: Dorling Kindersley, 2000), pp. 16–27; Clay, pp. 365–367, 381–392; Wyden, pp. 189–194.

pp. 13–17: *Current Biography* (hereafter *CB*) (New York: H. W. Wilson) 1952, pp. 602–604 (Ulbricht entry); Carola Stern, *Ulbricht: A Political Biography*, trans. Abe Farbstein (New York: Praeger, 1965), pp. 5–6, 200–201; Cate, pp. 27–29, 35; *FoF* 1953, pp. 194–195, 204; David E. Murphy, Sergei A. Kondrashev, and George Bailey, *Battleground Berlin: CIA vs. KGB in the Cold War* (New Haven, Conn.: Yale University Press, 1997), pp. 163–169; Joseph J. Trento, *The Secret History of the CIA* (Roseville, Calif.: Prima, 2001), pp. 101–104.

pp. 17–18: Honoré M. Catudal, *Kennedy and the Berlin Wall Crisis* (West Berlin: Berlin Verlag, 1980), pp. 40, 48–49, 210; Cate, pp. 26, 143;

Wyden, pp. 85–90; *FoF* 1961, pp. 278–280; Charles Wighton, *Adenauer—Democratic Dictator: A Critical Biography* (London: Muller, 1963), pp. 40–41, 328–331; Frank A. Mayer, *Adenauer and Kennedy: A Study in German-American Relations, 1961–1963* (New York: St. Martin's Press, 1996), p. 56.

pp. 18–22: Cate, pp. 22–23; *FoF* 1956, pp. 353–356, 364–367; Harold Macmillan, *Pointing the Way* (New York: Harper and Row, 1972), pp. 335–339, 348–350, 392, 403; Catudal, pp. 56–62, 274–275; "Vous êtes bien, Madame?" reported in conversation by Nicholas L. King; Brian Crozier, *De Gaulle* (New York: Charles Scribner's Sons, 1973), pp. 520, 527–529, 555–560.

pp. 22–24: *CB* 1949, pp. 5–7 (Adenauer entry); *FoF* 1954, 353–355.

pp. 24–32: Catudal, pp. 43, 69, 83–84, 141, 147–149, 151, 270–271, 276–278; Richard Reeves, *President Kennedy: Profile of Power* (New York: Simon and Schuster, 1993), pp. 113–114; Wyden, p. 174; Cate, p. 322; *CB* 1960, pp. 42–44 (Bohlen entry); *FoF* 1955, pp. 237–240; *FoF* 1959, pp. 309–310; *FoF* 1960, pp. 165, 327, 333–336; Strobe Talbott, ed., *Khrushchev Remembers: The Last Testament* (Boston: Little, Brown, 1974), pp. 407–413.

pp. 32–36: Catudal, pp. 82–83, 102–108, 110, 115–119; David Halberstam, *The Best and the Brightest* (New York: Random House, 1972), pp. 75–76; Wyden, pp. 49–50; Kenneth P. O'Donnell and David F. Powers, with Joe McCarthy, *Johnny, We Hardly Knew Ye: Memories of John Fitzgerald Kennedy* (New York: Pocket Books, 1973), p. 275; Cate, pp. 17–22; *New York Times* (hereafter *NYT*), June 7, 1961.

pp. 36–37: Wyden, p. 56; James Reston, *Deadline: A Memoir* (New York: Random House, 1991), pp. 290–291; Catudal, pp. 120, 122, 125; *NYT*, June 16, 1961; Cate, p. 62.

pp. 38–39: Catudal, pp. 143–150, 159; Cate, pp. 85–87; Wyden, pp. 73–76.

pp. 39–41: Catudal, pp. 164, 166; Cate, pp. 77, 98, 122, 125–127.

pp. 41–46: Wyden, p. 56; Catudal, pp. 176–177, 191–194, 197–202; *NYT*, July 26, 28, and 31, and August 3, 1961; Cate, pp. 108–115; Theodore C. Sorensen, *Kennedy* (New York: Harper and Row, 1965), pp. 591–592.

pp. 46–48: Cate, pp. 33–36; Wyden, pp. 388–391; Stern, p. 196.

pp. 48–54: Cate, pp. 139–145, 154–161, 517; Catudal, pp. 205, 211, 212.

pp. 54–55: Murphy, Kondrashev, and Bailey, pp. 6–12, 152–153, 457; Trento, pp. 69–70, 93–98, 140–146, 161–162, 177.

pp. 56–62: Catudal, pp. 23–28, 36–38, 227–230, 232–234; *NYT*, August 8 and 14, 1961; Cate, pp. 170–172, 175–177, 191, 236–248; Trento, pp. 185–188; Murphy, Kondrashev, and Bailey, pp. 363–364; Wyden, pp. 26–28, 78, 133–141, 168.

2: The Continuing Crisis

pp. 63–70: Catudal, pp. 32–33; Wyden, pp. 152, 157, 161–163, 176, 189–195, 214, 226–234; Cate, pp. 265–267, 276–277, 300–304, 350–351, 380–381, 402–413, 423–436, 458, 461–462; Mac-Donogh, p. 441; *CB* 1951, pp. 274–276 (Higgins entry); Clay, p. 361; *CB* 1945, pp. 111–114 (Clay entry); Hubert H. Humphrey, *The Education of a Public Man: My Life and Politics* (Garden City, N.Y.: Doubleday, 1976), p. 199.

pp. 70–75: Cate, pp. 15, 140–141, 219, 312–314, 341–342, 345, 363, 373, 379, 387, 438; Wyden, pp. 140, 221–222; Peter Claus Schmidt, director, *The Fall of the Berlin Wall* (Warner Home Video, 1990); Catudal, p. 132.

pp. 75–76: Cate, pp. 213, 288–289, 368–370, 377–378, 381, 438; *FoF* 1961, p. 347.

pp. 76–78: Cate, pp. 440–442, 448–449, 452, 457–458; Clay, pp. 13–15; Macmillan, pp. 392–395.

pp. 79–85: Cate, pp. 461–462, 467–470, 476–487, 492; Catudal, pp. 133–135, 197; Wyden, pp. 264, 271.

pp. 85–89: Cate, pp. 382–383; Wyden, pp. 273–274, 288–294; Schmidt, *Fall* (this video reproduces a short excerpt from Frank's film); *NYT*, December 12, 1962; *FoF* 1962, p. 273; Catudal, pp. 291–293; Francis Russell, "Second Thoughts on Peter Fechter," *National Review* (hereafter *NR*), November 20, 1962, p. 389.

pp. 89–92: Wyden, pp. 54–55, 276–279; James Burnham, "Intelligence on Cuba," *NR*, November 20, 1962, p. 386; Ronald Payne and Christopher Dobson, *Who's Who in Espionage* (New York: St. Martin's Press, 1984), pp. 129–131; *FoF* 1962, pp. 361–362; *NR Bulletin*, November 13, 1962, pp. 1–5.

3: In the Shadow of the Wall

pp. 93–95: *NR Bulletin,* July 9, 1963, p. 1; *FoF* 1963, pp. 233–234; Wyden, pp. 282–283; *NYT,* June 26 and 28, 1963.

pp. 95–96: *FoF* 1963, pp. 225, 314, 351.

pp. 96–101: Anthony Kemp, *Escape from Berlin* (London: Boxtree, 1987), pp. 68–81; Schmidt, *Fall.*

pp. 101–103: *FoF* 1963, pp. 152, 211, 295, 361, 367, 368, 375; *FoF* 1964, pp. 357–361; *CB* 1964, p. 118 (Erhard entry); *CB* 1967, p. 472 (Adenauer obituary); Trento, pp. 106–107, 279–280; *FoF* 1971, p. 721; Wyden, p. 284.

pp. 103–106: Wyden, pp. 297–308, 315–321, 324; *Green Guide, Germany (West Germany and Berlin)* (Clermont-Ferrand, France: Michelin, 1986), p. 73; Kemp, pp. 77–78; Schmidt, *Fall;* John O. Koehler, *Stasi: The Untold Story of the East German Secret Police* (Boulder, Colo.: Westview Press, 1999), p. 17.

pp. 106–108: Wyden, pp. 274–275, 308–314, 350–351, 557–559; James B. Donovan, *Strangers on a Bridge: The Case of Colonel Abel* (New York: Atheneum, 1964), pp. 318, 349–350, 371–375, 376–398, 417–420; Dobson and Payne, pp. 3–4, 105–106, 181–182.

pp. 108–111: Schmidt, *Fall;* Denise Noe, *The Baader–Meinhof Gang* (http://www.crimelibrary.com/terrorists/Baader/); Richard Huffman, *This Is Baader–Meinhof* (http://www.baader-meinhof.com/about/contact.htm); *FoF* 1977, pp. 789–791; *FoF* 1974, p. 952; MacDonogh, p. 423.

pp. 111–113: *FoF* 1968, pp. 203–205, 214, 235; Crozier, pp. 616–636; *FoF* 1969, pp. 219, 249.

pp. 113–116: *FoF* 1968, pp. 7, 119, 152, 163, 281, 305–306, 349–351, 369–370; *FoF* 1969, pp. 235, 682.

pp. 116–118: Wyden, pp. 222, 426–433, 438–447, photo section following 396; kettledrum reported in conversation by Jan Lukas; Schmidt, *Fall;* Jerry Bornstein, *The Wall Came Tumbling Down: The Berlin Wall and the Fall of Communism* (New York: Outlet, 1990), p. 13.

pp. 118–120: *FoF* 1969, pp. 621, 684; *FoF* 1965, p. 352; *FoF* 1966, pp. 470–471; Wyden, pp. 210–211, 352–354; *NR,* September 24, 1971, pp. 1046–1047; *FoF* 1970, pp. 87, 200; *FoF* 1971, pp. 651,

686–687; Henry Kissinger, *White House Years* (Boston: Little, Brown, 1979), pp. 410–412, 711–723, 806–808; *FoF* 1972, pp. 897–898, 1036.

pp. 121–122: *FoF* 1968, pp. 471–472; *CB* 1952, pp. 602–604 (Ulbricht entry); *FoF* 1971, pp. 338, 935; *CB* 1972, pp. 227–230 (Honecker entry); *CB* 1973, p. 463 (Ulbricht obituary).

pp. 122–126: *CB* 1992, p. 628 (Brandt obituary); *FoF* 1971, p. 860; Murphy, Kondrashev, and Bailey, pp. 135–138, 300; Basile Tesselin, *Guillaume, l'espion tranquille du chancelier* (Paris: France-empire, 1979), pp. 39–41, 105, 147, 157–174, 192–201; Koehler, pp. 151–163; Markus Wolf with Anne McElroy, *Man without a Face* (New York: PublicAffairs, 1997), pp. 166–186; Willy Brandt, *People and Politics: The Years 1960–1975*, trans. J. Maxwell Brownjohn (Boston: Little, Brown, 1978), pp. 13–20, 450; Dobson and Payne, pp. 68–69; *FoF* 1974, p. 374; *FoF* 1975, pp. 854–855.

pp. 126–128: Wyden, pp. 566, 608–609, 672–673; Kemp, pp. 30, 162; Schmidt, *Fall;* Bornstein, pp. 13, 28; Terry Tillman, *The Writings on the Wall: Peace at the Berlin Wall* (Santa Monica, Calif.: 22/7 Publishing, 1990), passim.

pp. 128–131: *NYT* "Week in Review," May 8, 1988; B. Jicinski, "'That Slanderous Pamphlet,'" *NR,* April 1, 1977, p. 383; *FoF* 1952, pp. 370, 390; *FoF* 1978, pp. 17, 180, 635, 749, 868; *FoF* 1981, pp. 44, 81, 921–922, 947; *CB* 1981, pp. 436–439 (Walesa entry); *CB* 1982, pp. 171–172 (Jaruzelski entry); Peter Schweizer, ed., *The Fall of the Berlin Wall: Reassessing the Causes and Consequences of the End of the Cold War* (Stanford, Calif.: Hoover Institution Press, 2000), p. 22.

pp. 131–135: Schweizer, pp. 54–56, 69–76; Kemp, pp. 159–162; Wyden, pp. 566, 568, 605–606; Bornstein, pp. 16–17; Ronald Reagan, *An American Life* (New York: Simon and Schuster, 1990), pp. 680–683; *NYT,* June 12 and 13, 1987; Schmidt, *Fall;* Fox News special, "Tear Down This Wall" (October 19, 2002).

4: The Wall Came Tumbling Down

pp. 137–144: *FoF* 1989, pp. 26, 111–112, 148, 202, 244, 273, 423–424, 485, 607, 613; Wyden, pp. 629–631, 681; *FoF* 1988, pp. 206, 217, 385–386, 435, 445, 473, 474, 519, 840–842, 885, 918, 936; *CB*

1996, p. 616 (Walesa entry); *FoF* 1987, pp. 905–910, 983; *NYT*, August 8 and 21, 1989; Schweizer, pp. 27–34.

pp. 144–148: Cate, p. 94; *FoF* 1989, pp. 71, 186, 299, 300, 313, 331, 332, 394, 402–403, 434, 643; Wyden, p. 604; Schweizer, pp. 27–34; Murphy, Kondrashev, and Bailey, p. 397; Wolf, p. 250.

pp. 148–153: *FoF* 1989, pp. 343, 590–591, 659–660, 677–678, 747; Bornstein, pp. 18–19, 63, 67–68; Schmidt, *Fall;* *NYT,* September 29 and 30, and October 1, 1989.

pp. 153–156: *FoF* 1989, pp. 112, 343, 463–464, 624; *FoF* 1956, p. 365; *NYT,* August 22, 1989.

pp. 156–159: *FoF* 1989, pp. 254, 520, 757, 764–765, 785–786, 915; Schmidt, *Fall;* Bornstein, pp. 18, 20; *CB* 1990, p. 377 (Krenz entry); Wolf, p. xxvi.

pp. 159–161: *FoF* 1989, pp. 820–822; *Encyclopaedia Britannica,* 15th ed. (Chicago: Encyclopaedia Britannica, 1985), Vol. 7, p. 907 (Tomas Masaryk entry); *FoF* 1948, pp. 77–78, 87, 282; *NYT,* October 30, 1989.

pp. 161–163: *CB* 1990, pp. 375–379 (Krenz entry); *FoF* 1989, pp. 830–831.

pp. 163–167: Schmidt, *Fall;* *FoF* 1989, p. 829; Bennett Owen, "The Party at the Wall," *NR,* December 22, 1989, pp. 20–21; Bornstein, pp. 21–26, 58; *NYT,* November 11, 1989; Tillman, passim.

pp. 167–174: *FoF* 1989, pp. 243, 292, 853, 864–865, 879, 885–886, 925, 957–959, 976, 977; *NYT,* November 22, 1989; Anthony Daniels, "Curtain Still Down," *NR,* December 22, 1989, pp. 21–23; Bornstein, p. 73; http://archives.tcm.ie/breakingnews/2001/01/20/story2089.asp; http://www.timisoara.com/timisoara/rev/trialscript.html.

pp. 175–178: *FoF* 1989, pp. 863, 894, 914–915, 931–932, 947–948, 977–978; *CB* 1990, p. 379 (Krenz entry); Bornstein, p. 83; Schmidt, *Fall.*

5: The End of the Cold War

pp. 179–181: *NR,* January 27, 1989; Radek Sikorski, "Poland's Good Old Days (Now)," *NR,* December 22, 1989, pp. 23–24; Milton Friedman, "Four Steps to Freedom," *NR,* May 14, 1990, pp. 33–36.

pp. 181–185: Wyden, pp. 604, 609, 669–671; *FoF* 1990, pp. 33–34, 106, 138, 144, 145, 185, 264–265, 733, 736; Koehler, pp. 406–409; *Berlin* (Dorling Kindersley), p. 165.

pp. 186–188: Koehler, pp. 8–9, 407–411; *FoF* 1990, p. 915; Wolf, pp. xxi–xxii, 375–379, 386; Kemp, pp. 46–48; Bornstein, pp. 90–92.

pp. 189–192: Wolf, pp. 5–6; *FoF* 1991, pp. 36–37, 176, 225, 404, 414–415, 526, 621–622, 637, 929.

Index